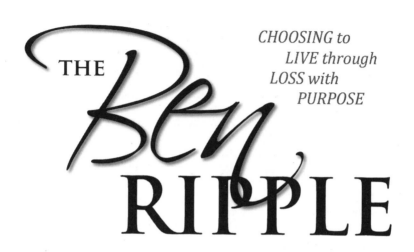

THE

Ben

RIPPLE

CHOOSING to LIVE through LOSS with PURPOSE

LISA ELLIOTT

THE BEN RIPPLE

Copyright © 2012 by Lisa Elliott

Printed in Canada

ISBN:978-1-77069-430-9

Word Alive Press
131 Cordite Road, Winnipeg, MB R3W 1S1
www.wordalivepress.ca

WORD ALIVE PRESS
Just Write!

Library and Archives Canada Cataloguing in Publication

Elliott, Lisa, 1963-
    The Ben ripple / Lisa Elliott.

ISBN 978-1-77069-430-9

    1. Elliott, Benjamin, 1990-2009. 2. Elliott, Lisa, 1963-
3. Lymphoblastic leukemia--Patients--Biography. 4. Lymphoblastic leukemia--Patients--Religious life. 5. Suffering--Religious aspects--Christianity. I. Title.

RC643.E45 2011   616.99'419092   C2011-907577-6

DEDICATION

BENJAMIN DAVID ELLIOTT
JUNE 30, 1990–AUGUST 19, 2009

Well, Ben, who would've thought that all of those rambling thoughts of mine would end up being published one day? I can still picture you sitting there at my side rolling your eyes at me, asking me what I was telling the world about you this time. It always gave me great pleasure when you threw in your own two cents' worth. I can only imagine what your words are worth now in light of eternity!

Hopefully God has given you a good view to see how He's using your life to *ripple* out for His glory. I love ya, Bud! I miss you every single day! I'm looking forward to the day when we all join you for that eternal party in heaven!

Mom
(Dzumus)

TABLE OF CONTENTS

ACKNOWLEDGEMENTS

To begin with, I'd like to thank our medical team, the nurses and staff at the London Health Sciences Centre, as well as our VON nurses, for being such an incredible source of support, care, and love toward me and my family. You transcended the call of duty to make personal investments in our lives, and you will forever hold a special place in our hearts.

Thank you to all of the Facebook followers, who so faithfully prayed and sojourned with us every step of the way. Thank you for planting the seed in my mind to consider publishing my journey.

Thank you to our close friends and our immediate, extended, and church families for your patient and sacrificial love toward me and my family through the darkest time of our lives. Thank you for sustaining us with your ever-creative and practical expressions of love. You taught me how to do it right! And you can be sure that I've taken good notes!

Thank you to Andrew, Joy, and Heather for agreeing to weed through my countless updates. Your gracious reviews gave me the confidence I needed to take it to the next level.

Thank you to Shelly Esser, my editor extraordinaire and sister of the heart. Thank you for your unmerited invested interest in me. I am not only humbled by your encouragement to publish my journey, but also by your eager willingness to come alongside me to make it a reality. Your professional insight, godly counsel, validation, sensitivity, and prayers have been invaluable. Thank you for patiently guiding me, ever so gently, to take baby steps toward making my mess my message.

Thank you to all those at Word Alive Press who believed enough in my manuscript to put it in print. What an incredible opportunity you've afforded me! I'm praying that you, too, will reap eternal *ben*efits as you meet up with the lives that have been changed as a result of your willingness to join me in my journey!

Thank you to my husband, David. You are the love of my life! Who would have thought when we began our journey together twenty-five years ago that the path would lead us through the valley of the shadow of the death of one of our children? Over the years, we have parented together, ministered together, and grown together, but most importantly, we've stuck together. Thank you for lovingly encouraging me to surrender it all for God's glory.

Finally, thank you to my Lord and Savior, Jesus Christ. You are carrying me from strength to strength. You are my source of inspiration, inexpressible joy, incomprehensible peace, and only hope. To You alone be the glory to the ends of the earth!

PREFACE

This was never intended to be a book. Rather, it began as a raw journal, written to help me process my personal thoughts through the illness and subsequent death of my son Ben, after his year-long battle with leukemia. At the request of a friend, I began to send brief updates relaying the bare essentials to a few interested people.

As public interest grew, so too did the response of those who joined our journey. I began to hear daily from complete strangers, those who were on their own cancer journey, were dealing with health problems, or were involved in their own pain management and life issues. These people evidently were not only reading, but entering into and looking forward to my updates as a source of hope, encouragement, and inspiration in their own lives. In fact, it's largely because of the thousands of people who faithfully stuck with us through our journey, encouraging me to put it into publication, that you hold this book in your hands.

In the pages to follow, you will find excerpts from my own personal journal, Scriptures that served as lifelines to keep my head above water while the waves of crisis threatened to drown me, practical insights I have learned along the way, and also selected updates that I relayed to a watching and waiting world as I lived out my worst nightmare.

It could be that you have picked this book up as one who has or is dealing with the loss of a child. Perhaps you've experienced a family crisis like mine. You will undoubtedly feel the pain a little more acutely than others as you journey with me. As much as this book is full of words, I have no words that can possibly ease your pain.

Or perhaps you are facing pain and loss of a different kind. Maybe it's not the illness or loss of a child, but rather the death of a dream. Maybe you've experienced the loss of a job or a significant relationship. Loss is loss, after all.

You may not be presently going through any particular loss or crisis. Rather, your desire may be to genuinely and sensitively come alongside someone else who is.

Whoever you are, from wherever you are, in whatever circumstance or loss you're facing, I am thankful that our paths have crossed. It's my hope that in the pages to follow you will find validation, comfort, encouragement, insights, and the practical tools you need to take the next step on your own journey.

Letting it ripple for the glory of God,

Lisa Elliott

INTRODUCTION

We are all only one phone call away from our lives changing forever. I received my phone call at work on August 12, 2008. It was from my husband, David, on his way to the hospital emergency room with our eighteen-year-old son, Ben, who had collapsed at work.

Ben was carrying a bucket of ice across the restaurant where he was serving tables when he suddenly couldn't catch his breath. After being encouraged to sit down for a moment, he was unable to get back up again. It was then that Ben's co-worker called David to come and pick him up. Ben insisted that he simply needed to go home to rest. However, his athletic frame failed to climb the three steps into our home, and when he was uncharacteristically brought to tears, David's fatherly instincts took charge.

I would only have to wait for half an hour before receiving another phone call. This time David told me that blood work had come back showing an abnormally low hemoglobin level of 42 (normal for Ben's age and size is 180). As much as I tried to focus on anything in the office that would serve to distract me, I could do nothing but sit, staring blindly into space while I continued to wait for anything indicating that I should go to the hospital.

Within the hour, a third phone call informed me that doctors were going to perform a bone marrow biopsy, a painful procedure where bone marrow is retrieved via a long coring instrument inserted into the hip bone. I told my husband to come and get me.

The Ben Ripple

When our vehicle pulled up only minutes later, one look into David's face told me everything I needed to know for the time being. An ominous feeling came over us as we quietly and tearfully made our way back to the hospital, where the bone marrow biopsy was already underway.

In the moments that followed, I struggled to make sense of all that was unfolding. Ben was the second oldest of our four children. He was making plans to run a victory lap at his high school in three weeks as captain of the volleyball team. His goal was to complete a few extra courses required to enter the nursing program at university the next fall. He had just played a round of golf with his dad two days before. And hadn't he just ridden his bike to work that morning?

Now standing in the chemotherapy treatment wing of the local hospital, we were told that there was some erratic cell behavior, and they were checking into the possibility of leukemia.

So this was it. This was the moment I'd heard countless others speak about—the moment when what was happening really couldn't be happening. This was the kind of moment only *someone else* experienced.

Up until this moment, our lives were full of the typical stuff of life. My husband and I had been happily married for twenty-two years. Our home was a host for all the activity and demands that go with being in full-time pastoral ministry. Together we had raised four healthy and happy children, who were just beginning to spread their wings and find the independence we had trained them for.

While everything inside me seemed to be moving in slow motion, activity around me abruptly accelerated. Blood transfusions were initiated, medications were administered, and plans were made to get Ben to a cancer care treatment center located an hour from our home.

David left me with Ben while he picked up our youngest daughter, Erin (fourteen), from school. Upon her arrival, she could hardly bring herself to enter Ben's hospital room for fear of what she had to face beyond the door. We would have to wait until later on that day to call Natalie (nineteen) and Jacob (sixteen), who were both working at camps, three hours away in opposite directions. How would they respond? And then there was Ben's girlfriend, Sarah, who had been unsuspectingly working in the hospital kitchen just two floors below. Now watching her silently sob at Ben's bedside, we tried to take in our new reality. There were many more tears as family and friends joined us in our surreal state.

I felt as if I'd been heavily sedated, yet somehow expected to function. I knew I needed to eat something to sustain me through my worst nightmare, so a friend walked me down to the hospital café. Indecision overwhelmed me as I scanned the menu on the wall behind the counter. I wasn't even sure what would appeal and wondered, with the nausea that welled within me, if anything I decided upon would even stay down. My friend finally made the decision for me, and we took a bowl of soup outside the hospital, where I could get some much needed air.

I sat playing with my spoon, waiting for my brain to signal my hand to raise it to my lips. Even my tears seemed to flow down my cheeks in slow motion. I sat staring into the clear sunny sky through a thick fog that now encompassed me and threatened to swallow me whole.

This was the day when my world stood still.

CHAPTER 1

Out OF CONTROL

After everyone else had left and we got Ben settled, David, Erin, and I apprehensively left him alone in the hospital for the night. Once home, we were finally able to get in touch with our other two children, Jacob and Natalie. Their responses were pretty much what we expected—stunned silence, tears, questions, and all that the rest of us had experienced in the hours before.

Sleep didn't come easily for any of us as we tried to wrap our minds around what was happening. Our strong, healthy Ben had *what* disease? In the middle of the night, Erin crawled into our queen-sized bed, and the three of us lay quietly sobbing in a suffocated mournful harmony. When sleep didn't come we got up, put a pot of coffee on, and wandered aimlessly around the house.

Was there anything that had indicated the onset of this deadly disease? Ben had been complaining of some shortness of breath, chest pain, and lethargy for about a month. We remembered a couple of recent all-day nose bleeds. On one occasion, he cut his finger with our cheese grater and couldn't stop the bleeding. The week before, he had to get off of his bike on the way home from work to sit down and catch his breath. Another day he was unable to cut the grass as a result of his fatigue, and during a family excursion to the beach he got chilled with no hope of getting warm again. We mulled things over and over again in our minds until they hurt. And when we couldn't wait any longer, we returned to the hospital, where we were told that Ben would be transported to the cancer care treatment center later that day.

1

The Ben Ripple

Having just turned eighteen six weeks earlier, Ben was admitted into the adult ward at the cancer care treatment center as their youngest patient. As nurses took charge to get him situated, I began to shuffle down the hallway at a pace I wouldn't exceed for the next year. The walls were lined with pictures "in memory of." I couldn't imagine that we were now a part of this grim neighborhood, but for the time being I wouldn't allow my mind to go to the dark places that might lead to adding Ben's face to those walls one day.

Within the next twenty-four hours, Ben was diagnosed with ALL (Acute Lymphoblastic Leukemia), a form of leukemia typically found in children ages two to five. This hospital was going to be Ben's home for at least the next month to commence what was to be a two-and-a-half-year treatment plan.

It amazed me just how easily our busy and full lives could come to an abrupt stop to allow for crises such as the one we now faced as a family. Suddenly everything revolved around Ben's illness. Our lives were completely spinning out of control!

We had to quickly take inventory and make the necessary arrangements to accommodate for this unforeseen and unimaginable twist in the road. To begin with, although he never came right out and said it, it became immediately clear that Ben didn't want to be left alone during the night. So David took the night-shift at Ben's side on a pullout bed-chair while Erin and I stayed at my aunt's home just twenty minutes away.

The next morning, Erin and I headed back to the hospital. I asked how Ben's night was. David reported that all had been well until Ben was awakened at 1:00 a.m. by a nosebleed that wouldn't stop. Then he was up vomiting at 6:00 a.m. It occurred to me that these were the same times I had been awakened by similar symptoms! This could be no coincidence. Rather, I believe it was God's way of letting me know that Ben wasn't alone on this journey. We were all in this together. The question was, how would we survive?

I had been prayer-journaling for years as a way to record, process, and apply truths and principles from God's Word to my life. If there was a time in my life that I needed to record, process, and apply, it was now. So I poured out my heart to the One who knew my thoughts before there was a word on my tongue.

• • •

PRAYER JOURNAL ENTRY
Sunday, August 17, 2008

Here I sit in Ben's hospital room. I'm in a cerebral mode today, so I'm able to function.

Ben's doing okay. He's experienced some nausea due to the antibiotic this morning. He's also become hypersensitive to scents of any kind.

As of yesterday, I've moved into an "in the moment" coping mode. If I think too deeply about life as we knew it just last week, it's brutal. I can't imagine what tomorrow, let alone the next week, looks like. I have to maintain hope for the future while also coming to terms with our new reality.

But even "in the moment," it feels surreal. I feel like I'm talking about someone else's life. I haven't totally grasped the fact that Ben won't be coming home this weekend once he feels better.

Lifeline

> "I will lie down and sleep in peace, for you alone, O Lord, make me dwell in safety" (Psalm 4:8).

• • •

Amid the numerous adjustments and inconveniences, we experienced a strange settling effect and sense of comfort in our new sterile and foreign environment. Nurses immediately took a liking to Ben. His nurse practitioner, Susan, endearingly and possessively claimed him as "my boy," checking in on him every chance she had. Aware that Ben was planning on pursuing a nursing degree, she began to make a vocabulary list on his whiteboard and kidded with him that he could likely complete his first year of studies by the time his treatment was finished. And so our education began!

Over the days that followed, Ben and his dad eagerly read through the information booklet we'd been given, which told us everything we needed to know about the disease, the treatment plan, and medications and such. They spent hours surfing the Internet to learn all they could about leukemia.

Meanwhile, *my* time on the Internet was spent familiarizing myself with the latest social network on Facebook. Up until now, Facebook had only been a means to keep up with my oldest daughter, Natalie, while she was away at college. Who would have thought that such a trendy phenomenon would grow to be a social lifeline, becoming my primary source of communication with the outside world for the months to follow?

Soon after word got out about Ben's illness, I was contacted by a friend. She told me that she had created a Facebook group and called it "Prayer for Benjamin Elliott." Her thinking was that this would be a more manageable way for me to communicate with those who wanted to be kept in the know. The group grew in number daily and included hundreds within weeks!

The irony was that while David and Ben continued to immerse themselves in their research, I could hardly form the word *leukemia* on my lips, let alone bear the responsibility as the translator of this new foreign language to the watching and waiting world! My initial messages were simple and to the point. There was no use confusing anyone with medical terms, statistics, and details that we ourselves were just getting acquainted with. The first update read,

• • •

Prayer for Benjamin Elliott
Monday, August 18, 2008
So here's the scoop. For now, we're looking at a month of intense chemotherapy—twenty-three days total, today being day three—so this hospital is our home for the month. We've also got a hotel room across the parking lot from the hospital that someone is anonymously footing the bill for. One of us will be staying at the hotel while the other stays at Ben's bedside every night.

This phase of the treatment is finished on September 11 (suitably 9-1-1), so we're hoping that God will grant remission on that day when his progress is tested via another bone marrow aspiration. We'll take inventory at that point and carry on from there.

The nursing staff is phenomenal!

We had a good day today. Ben was up for a shower and a walk down the hall, and we played a card game.

God is good, and I'm taking good notes of all He has to teach me through this time. His faithfulness is new every morning! Praise the Lord!

From God's waiting room,

Lisa (Ben's Mom)

PRAYER JOURNAL ENTRY
Wednesday, August 20, 2008

Today I was left alone with Ben for the first time since his diagnosis. I went and stood by the window overlooking our new neighborhood.

As tears slowly made their way down my face, it began to rain. I can't help but think that You were crying with me, Lord. I could tell by the look of the sky that it was going to be an all-day kind of rain.

Taking note of my tears, Ben handed me his iPod. He encouraged me to listen to the song he had playing. It was the group Casting Crowns, singing "Praise You in This Storm." Something tells me that I'm going to have to do just that—learn to praise You, Lord, through the biggest storm of my life.

• • •

And what a storm it was turning out to be!

• • •

PRAYER JOURNAL ENTRY
Thursday, August 21, 2008

Today, the doctor came in and informed us that more blood work has come back indicating that Ben has a rare chromosome shift/translocation of cells. This puts him into a high-risk category, meaning that it is highly unlikely that he will go into remission and very likely that, if and when he does, he will have a relapse. Each member of our family will have to have genetic blood testing to see if any one of us is a bone marrow match for an inevitable transplant. It is a blow, for sure!

• • •

Looking at Ben sitting up in his new surroundings bright-eyed and smiling made it hard to fathom that he was as sick as we were being told he was. As I sat on the end of the hospital bed, trying to catch the breath that had just been sucked out of me, Ben asked, "How are you doing, Mom?"

"Not well," I told him.

We sat quietly for a few more minutes until I realized how selfish it was of me to wallow in my own self-pity while he, the patient, sought to comfort me! So, setting aside my own feelings, I asked him in turn, "How are you doing, Ben?"

"Well, there's nothing much you can do about it!" he replied with a shrug.

As our journey unfolded, Ben often translated this phrase into an abbreviated form, saying, "Whatever." It was not the cry of a victim. Rather, it became obvious to us that this was his verbal way of accepting circumstances that were well beyond his control.

• • •

Prayer for Benjamin Elliott
Friday, August 22, 2008
So far, Ben's had two allergic reactions to the drugs he's been administered. In response to one of his antibiotics, he got a case of the rigors (shakes), and in response to an anti-nauseate, he reacted with stiffening and contortions. He also feels dizzy from another medication. Fortunately, all of these have been resolved with alternate treatment.

God's mercies are new every morning! Great is His faithfulness!
From God's waiting room,
Lisa (Mom)

• • •

Standing aside to helplessly watch Ben's reactions was alarming, to say the least—not only for each one of us, but also for Ben. During one of Ben's more severe reactions, Jacob and I left the hospital room to take a breath in the lounge. As we sat together sharing a box of Kleenex, a pigeon landed on the window ledge and strutted back and forth. He watched us closely the entire time. I told Jacob that it must have been God's way of letting us know that He was with us and wouldn't take His watchful eye off us.

Interest rose quickly, and there were more watchful eyes on us than we realized. It became obvious how well-liked Ben was. Many of his friends wanted to come and hang out at the hospital. Our church family and friends also wanted access to express their love and support. Then, of course, there was all of our extended family, most from out of town, wanting to help in whatever way they could.

We truly appreciated everyone's interest. However, what no one could understand were the many challenges of orchestrating all the comings and goings while keeping some sense of control.

• • •

PRAYER JOURNAL ENTRY
Saturday, August 23, 2008

Today we have had fourteen visitors!

Unfortunately, Ben isn't up for much talking and socializing, especially now that he's the topic of conversation. He has never been big on being the center of attention, not to mention being on display for those interested in getting upfront and personal. Besides, being weak and nauseous a lot of the time doesn't leave him up for entertaining guests.

As of today, we have decided to use code words and signals if people happen to drop in or overstay their welcome. These will be my cue to nicely encourage our guests to leave. Ben will let me know ahead of time what he's up for and how long he wants to visit. That way, there are no surprises, and I can set boundaries early on in the visit.

Despite how he feels, Ben is a courteous host. However, it's obvious after company leaves that he is emotionally and socially exhausted. Not to mention the added strain it puts on David and me as we seek to accommodate everyone with the grace required. I have hardly spoken to David outside of the hospital room since we began this journey over a week and a half ago. Fortunately, we both understand and realize the stress we're under and the fact that it's bound to show its ugly head between the two of us from time to time.

How are we going to survive this ride, Lord? How am I going to find balance with the visitors who show up to support us and yet, in light of Ben's condition, we have to turn away? How will I know when a visit goes too long? How will we prevent ourselves from bedside burnout?

Lifeline

> "Then each went to his own home. But Jesus went to the
> Mount of Olives" (John 7:53–8:1).

PRAYER JOURNAL ENTRY
Friday, August 29, 2008

It's the end of another day. Heaviness eventually set in, and it felt like I was crying all day, although I held back for the sake of all those around (and there were many). I eventually leaked with David. It felt good to get it out. I'm still living in the moment.

We've heard from so many people who are praying for us and giving a lot of practical support. However, the comings and goings of those who want to care and show their support by visiting is exhausting and draining.

I think I'll write a book one day to contribute to the Berenstain Bear collection and call it *Too Much Company*!

I'm afraid I'm not up to being a very good hostess as I provide *hospitality*.

Prayer for Benjamin Elliott
Saturday, August 30, 2008
Ben's had a good day after a good night's sleep… finally. Thank you all for your prayers in that regard. He was able to get out for a little fresh air today, and even got in a little nap this afternoon (which hasn't happened very often due to all the visitors and hospital activity).

Ben has a new "do." His random hair loss was getting a little messy and uncomfortable to sleep on. The "magic tricks" he performs for his guests by pulling out clumps of hair are making him look more like a convict than a cancer patient! So David, Erin, and I had the hair-buzzing ceremony last night with two of the nurses.

Continue to pray for our family as we go for our genetic blood tests this Wednesday to see if any of us are a bone marrow match for Ben. Erin, in particular, is a little nervous about this procedure, so if you could just add an extra dose of prayer on her behalf, we'd be grateful.

Thanks to all of you for your continued encouragement and prayer support. We couldn't do this without you! And, of course, we couldn't do it without our Sovereign Lord's constant presence and watchful care over us every step of this journey that we've only just begun.

From God's waiting room,
Lisa (Mom)

Prayer Journal Entry
Thursday, September 4, 2008
So much is out of our control. I'm seeing more and more clearly just how much control is important to us. And more and more I'm seeing how little control we have.

Lord, our lives are in Your hands. You are sovereign. You hold the future. You know the beginning from the end. We want to make plans. We want to know what lies ahead. Lord, help me continue to take life one minute at a time.

Lifeline

> "In his heart a man plans his course, but the Lord determines his steps" (Proverbs 16:9).

Prayer for Benjamin Elliott
Friday, September 5, 2008
Fast Breaking News and a *Huge* Praise the Lord!

We found out that Ben is in remission! That means we're on the road to the next phase of his treatment plan.

Thanking you, as always, for your ongoing prayers and support through this roller-coaster ride we've come to know as "life in God's waiting room."

Lisa (Mom)

• • •

Although I didn't doubt that God could, I knew based on all we'd been told regarding Ben's high-risk disease that remission simply meant that the leukemia was sleeping and we needed to do all we could to prevent it from waking up. Therefore, we felt it wise and important to follow the doctors' orders and do all they advised—though I must say, it wasn't for lack of those who had their own advice to give. Talk about out of control!

• • •

Prayer Journal Entry
Saturday, September 6, 2008
The word "remission" at this point feels about as surreal as "leukemia" did initially. I'd be lying if I said it doesn't scare me. There's always the chance of relapse, and no doubt there will be downers and surprises to come.

That's just life, though, isn't it, Lord? There is still a long road ahead of us, but I believe that You'll guide us day by day. I trust You, Lord.

I have quickly realized why You have removed me from most social settings and made my main form of communication through cyberspace. I'm not sure what my face-to-face reaction would be to those who don't hesitate to share their wealth of information. Everyone is suddenly a leukemia specialist! Ugh! I'm hearing things like "Thankfully, Ben has the good kind of leukemia!" I've been quoted statistics as to Ben's odds for survival. I have been given a number of ways to boost his immune system. (This, in particular, would be detrimental to Ben's condition rather than helpful as we are told that in light of the fact that this is a cancer of the immune system we need to suppress it, not boost it.) I've been told countless success stories as if, in our unique set of circumstances, I am supposed to find comfort in them. I am regularly given special diets and scolded for allowing Ben to eat various foods when he should be eating boiled, mashed asparagus for breakfast and a bedtime snack. (Meanwhile, we are happy when Ben is able to eat anything at all!) I have been given the latest "cure-all" hot off the presses of cancer cell development news. A few have gone as far as to declare that remission means that God has cured Ben. We just need to believe and have faith!

I personally don't see this as being a case for faith, as if our faith or lack thereof somehow obligates You to make our wishes come true. At the same time, Lord, I know You are able.

Lifeline

"Now to him who is able to do immeasurably more than all we ask or imagine, according to his power that is at work within us, to him be glory in the church and in Christ Jesus throughout all generations, for ever and ever! Amen" (Ephesians 3:20-21).

Bedside Manners

To help kill some time one day, Ben and I came up with a list of what to do and what not to do when it came to hospital visitation. We shared some frustrations, but fortunately also some good laughs, as we began to rehearse the visits of some who definitely needed an education.

- Always call ahead. Warning is good, and so is anticipation.
- Do not overstay your welcome. Set a limit verbally and stick to it. For example, "I'm only going to stay for fifteen minutes." Most experts recommend a short hospital visit of ten to fifteen minutes. It is much better to leave the patient wanting more of you than less.
- Take the initiative to leave rather than putting the responsibility on the patient to let you know when he or she has had enough.
- Be sensitive to the mood/situation/atmosphere surrounding the person you're visiting.
- Use common sense. If you have any sign of a cold or flu, please stay away until you're feeling better.
- Don't be afraid to express emotions. Tears can be comforting and validating.
- Offer specific, practical help and resources rather than just leaving it open for the person in need to figure it out and let you know. They may not even know what they need. For example: meals, carting kids around, yard work, housecleaning, etc.
- Make yourself available by checking in by phone every so often.
- Allow the person you're visiting to express his or her feelings regarding the situation without you judging or advising.
- When you don't know what to say... just say so: "There are no words." It's more important that you're present and that you simply listen.

11

CHAPTER 2

THE

New
NORMAL

News of Ben's remission meant we could finally go home! There was just one catch: before he could be discharged, he had to undergo minor brain surgery to insert what they called an Ommaya (pronounced *o-my-a*) reservoir into the top of his head. Oh, my aching heart! This is a small device, approximately one inch in diameter, that resembles a small flying saucer with a three-inch stem extending from the bottom of it. The stem is fed through a ventricle in the brain to administer chemotherapy straight into the central nervous system. The alternative was to undergo numerous lumbar punctures, a painful procedure by which a large needle injects chemotherapy into the lower spine.

Ben's surgery went well, and we were sent home to live a "normal" life, whatever that was supposed to mean. What does a normal life look like with a cancer patient? Never mind that the patient was my son!

Well-intentioned people made comments like "It must be so nice to finally be home!" They couldn't know that home was no longer the safe haven I had worked so hard to create for my family. Rather, it was a scary, lonely, isolated drop-in center where I worked madly to keep meals healthy; kitchen equipment, countertops, surfaces, and bathrooms sterile and sanitary; and the house at large as germ-free as possible. We actually set up a welcome station (if truth be told, a roadblock) right at our front door with a bottle of hand sanitizer accompanied by a sign that said, "Please Don't Forget to Wash Your Hands."

The Ben Ripple

There was no way to properly convey to anyone who hadn't experienced the security of the hospital after an entire month how unnerving it was to be "discharged." My mind was filled with "what ifs." What if Ben gets a fever? What if we can't get him back to the hospital in time before he goes septic? What if he has some weird reaction? What if things go south?

I had picked up a catchphrase in the devastating aftermath of the terrorist attack on the Twin Towers that took place in New York City on September 11, 2001. One woman in an interview said, "New York City will never be the same again! I guess we'll all have to get used to the new normal." Not only was the date of our transition significant, as it drew closer to the anniversary of 9/11, but I also knew that life as we knew it would never be the same. This was our "new normal."

• • •

Prayer for Benjamin Elliott
Tuesday, September 9, 2008
After living at the hospital with Ben over the past month, we were finally able to bring him home late yesterday afternoon. As Dorothy in *The Wizard of Oz* put it so well, "There's no place like home!" (Or is there?)

Of course, the exciting news of his remission and homecoming doesn't at all imply that our journey is anywhere near to being over. In fact, we've only just begun.

Having said that, and having been assigned the role of "resident guard dog," there are a couple of things I want to make you aware of.

First of all, as much as we love you and as much as I'm sure many of you would love to see Ben (and ourselves), we need you to please call first if you're at all thinking of coming to visit.

This leads me to my second precaution: if you have any sign of cold, sore throat, headache, or especially the flu, infection, or fever, we discourage you from even considering coming. Once again, we love you, but…

Again, we thank you for all your continued thoughts, prayers, and practical expressions of love for us.

From God's waiting room,
Lisa (Mom)

Prayer for Benjamin Elliott
Wednesday, September 10, 2008

Okay, so I have to edit a little of my recent news from yesterday's report. A friend of mine told me this morning that it was an understatement to say that I've been nominated the "resident watch dog." She thought that "pit bull with pink lipstick" was better suited. Oh well, it's a dirty job, but somebody's gotta do it!

We've been able to enjoy a couple of almost normal days back at home as a little bit of a reprieve between treatments. It's been such a blessing to have all six of us sitting around the dinner table for two consecutive nights!

In His waiting room,

Lisa (Mom)

• • •

A big part of our new normal was making weekly, and often daily, trips to the cancer clinic. It was located just six floors below where we had made ourselves at home in the first month of Ben's illness. I will not soon forget our first visit to the clinic. As we took stock of our surroundings and the swarms of people filling the chairs in the various waiting areas, it didn't take long to figure out that Ben was notably the youngest patient.

Each patient sported varying fashions of wigs, headscarves, walkers, and wheelchairs—and each was assigned a beeper much like the ones you are assigned at a busy restaurant while you wait for a table to become available. Honking beepers would sporadically go off with a surround-sound effect. Ben and I often shared his iPod headset to help drown them out and pass the time.

I went prepared with a bag full of all sorts of goodies. It included Ben's countless bottles of pills, our ever-growing medical binder (where we kept record of inpatient and outpatient treatments), my day planner for booking new appointments, a Sudoku puzzle book for distraction, a compact Tetris game, a stash of mints and strong-flavored gum (to rid Ben of the salty-bitter taste of his PICC line flushes), and, of course, an assortment of snacks, as Ben's steroid-induced cravings dictated.

Our new normal was consumed with waiting for blood results, waiting for test results, waiting for appointments to be made, then waiting for the appointments to take place, waiting for treatments to be finished, waiting for prescriptions to be filled, waiting for various tests, then waiting for their results. On top of these waiting periods was the wait to find out if any member of our family could be a bone marrow donor. "Hurry up and wait" was quickly becoming our new theme song. As I waited to see God's will unfold, I determined that I would make the best of it, but I have to admit that it wasn't easy.

However, throughout our outpatient treatments and everywhere he went, Ben exuded an ever-present smile, mischievous twinkle, and selfless attitude. It therefore didn't take long to win over the newest members of our hospital family.

• • •

PRAYER JOURNAL ENTRY
Sunday September 11, 2008

This has been a *very long* day, moving from one waiting room to another for eight hours. Here I sit in a cancer clinic! Who'd have thought? I'm realizing how raw I am right now. A whole range of emotions and thoughts enter my mind—fear of the unknown, anxiety, a heightened need to control, a hint of anger, and sadness. I can hardly comprehend what life has become! It feels surreal, yet very real. I have a deep resolve and determination like I've never experienced before, but I also feel helpless and uncertain as I face the days ahead.

Ben's life has been flashing before my eyes a lot lately. I've had countless recollections of his growing-up years. I've been bombarded by floods of memories of him I've treasured in my heart. I remember him as a baby, with his relentless colic. Then as a toddler with his strong will, determination, and independence; I had my work cut out for me. He has always been so hard-working and intense, always thinking ahead, organized, and therefore frustrated with disorganized people. He has forever challenged me with his ever-thinking, inquisitive mind. (In fact, he's just asked me what I'm doing writing in my prayer journal in the middle of a cancer clinic.) Underlying all of these strong character traits, he's always been so thoughtful and sensitive.

As I think about our upcoming journey of potentially two and a half years, I already sense the need to have strength to endure. With each step we've taken, Ben's been put into a higher-risk category. Each leg of this journey is new and a little unnerving, I must say. Each new reaction and treatment is unsettling and very scary.

Father, as we enter deeper into the no-hope zone, help us to find our hope in You.

• • •

While only a couple of months earlier my day planner was creatively color-coded to keep track of everyone's busy schedule, it now recorded only blood counts, fevers, bowel movements, and vomit sessions. It also documented scheduled clinic appointments and times for weekly and eventually daily home visits from the VON (Victorian Order of Nurses). Keeping track of all of these things was crucial. There were chemo treatments, doctor checkups, and all kinds of symptoms to be on the lookout for as we all worked together to monitor Ben's health.

But aside from these routine appointments, Ben experienced all the innumerable complications, tests, and painful procedures that his illness dictated. We became all too familiar with the twists and turns of this unfamiliar road.

We soon discovered that our "new normal" was full of the "abnormal."

• • •

Prayer for Benjamin Elliott
Friday, September 12, 2008
Well, here's some news nobody's going to want to hear… Ben's been readmitted as of this afternoon.

Following his treatment yesterday at the cancer clinic as an outpatient, he began to experience some headache and intense muscle and joint discomfort. His temperature began rising this morning, which put us on red alert.

It's amazing how quickly abnormal life becomes the norm. It's great to know that no matter where we are, God is with us and is watching over us, and it's an absolute assurance to know that Ben is in His very capable hands.

As always, from God's waiting room,
Lisa (Mom)

Lifeline

"Look at the birds of the air; they do not sow or reap or store away in barns, and yet your heavenly Father feeds them. Are you not much more valuable than they?" (Matthew 6:26).

PRAYER JOURNAL ENTRY
Tuesday, September 16, 2008
Yesterday we were able to bring Ben home for the night. David just took him back to the hospital, but I'm staying home until we know for sure what's going

on with the Ommaya. I'm hoping they can be home by this afternoon for the "BENefit" volleyball game the high school is hosting to raise money to buy Ben a laptop computer.

Home again. It's weird, but on a day like today when the sun's shining, when I've been working in the kitchen doing "normal" life—hearing Ben, Natalie, Erin, Jacob, and Sarah laughing in the background as I prepared dinner for all of us last night—and after having spent a night in my own bed with David, life seems doable and normal.

It's when I stop to think about all that's going on that I realize how *not* normal it is. It's here where I trust You, Lord, knowing You are sovereign and in control and actually knew about all of this from the beginning of time.

• • •

Although the volleyball game went on as scheduled, Ben's attendance was not meant to be. In fact, I was in the gym where the game was about to start, awaiting David and Ben's arrival, when David called from the hospital to report yet another malfunction. Ben's second Ommaya insertion had failed, and now plans had to be made to have it removed permanently.

I hung up the phone and turned my attention back to the game. The game itself was excellent. I was so proud of Jacob and many of Ben's good friends and volleyball teammates for taking the court against the teachers, many who had taught Ben. Everything was okay as long as I didn't allow myself to think about *why* this game was going on in the first place.

• • •

PRAYER JOURNAL ENTRY
Wednesday, September 17, 2008
In my walk and talk with You, Lord, on my way from hotel to hospital this morning and as I was, yet again, playing over in my mind the past day's events of medical frustrations, I've decided I've got to let it go. The fact is, we're getting the care we need, and I trust that the timing of everything, including the delays, is because it's the way You planned it.

In John 11, both Mary and Martha blamed you for being too late to keep their brother from dying. Martha tells Jesus what is (Lazarus is dead), then tells Him what could have been: "If only you had been here, Lord, our brother wouldn't be dead." I can thank You at this point for being on time, but You'll have to give me the strength and ability to forgive if and when the time comes when You're not.

The good news is that Martha then goes on to tell Jesus what she believes still can be. "Even now, Lord, I believe…" That's what I call Faith Plus! However, in verse 39, when Jesus goes to act on what Martha herself has invited Him to do, by moving the stone away from the tomb, Martha tries to stop Him!

I guess where I relate is that I do believe You can still do things out of my jurisdiction and control simply because of Your power and sovereignty. Where I'll have to watch myself is when, in my own limited understanding, I see You doing something that doesn't make sense, that I don't try to prevent You from doing what only You can do…and what in effect I've invited You to do.

I once again need to focus on what *is* rather than on what *if* or what I believe should or could be. One day at a time? More like one minute at a time!

• • •

Our daily lives had become as unpredictable as the weather. We couldn't plan any further ahead than dinner on any given day. Even lunch was open for interruption. I began to learn what it is to live life in the moment.

I was struck with the impressions that God laid on my heart as I opened up to Him. Some of these impressions were so profound that I felt I had to begin sharing them openly with those who were praying for us in every moment of every day.

My next update was a turning point and changed my approach to how I relayed my updates.

• • •

Prayer for Benjamin Elliott
Friday, September 19, 2008
Our life has moved from living by the day to living one minute at a time.

Yesterday, as I spent time alone with the Lord and poured out my heart to Him, He laid some things on my heart that I feel are worth sharing with you all, to give you a window into the work He's doing in this mother's heart.

Living in the moment doesn't wallow in the land of "if only." It doesn't reflect on the past, in case seeds of bitterness and regrets are planted. These are bad weeds that will sap me of any true strength to deal with the task at hand.

19

Living in the moment doesn't live in the land of "what if." It doesn't forecast the future, in case seeds of worry, anxiety, and fear take root. Ninety percent of what we worry about never takes place anyway, so it's a waste of time and energy that I don't have to spare right now.

Living in the moment only requires what is needed at the time. It's dealing with what *is* rather than what should or could be, setting aside our "if onlys" or "what ifs."

Living in the moment means celebrating the process rather than regretting the past or putting things off until tomorrow (tomorrow, by the way, is not promised for any of us). It means taking time to celebrate with Natalie at her Summit Bible College graduation. It's celebrating Jacob's sixteenth birthday. It's celebrating Erin's back-to-school deals! It's celebrating Ben's first popcorn experience after a month's deprivation!

Living in the moment means making the best of today, this hour, this moment, since yesterday is history and tomorrow is a mystery. But here in this moment, today, is a gift, and that's why we call it the present.

Living in the moment means savoring each blessing that comes along.

Living in the moment means allowing tears to flow when the moment proves to be a painful one, and making sure to take time to taste the tears of the moment, as it's all one is able to endure at a time.

Living in the moment means living in the moment and trusting God with the bigger picture.

Living in the moment is where Jesus lives. He holds the future. He has a purpose for the past. Great *is* His faithfulness! His mercies are new every morning! This is the day that the Lord has made!

Thanks for sharing this moment with me,

Lisa (Mom)

• • •

As our journey unfolded, there was a growing interest in how Ben was doing, how things were going, and how we, as a family, were handling it. We kept as upbeat as we could in spite of everything, and we were all doing as well as possible under the circumstances. However, we didn't want to tell people "all is well" when in truth all was… "well?" I didn't personally see the point of sugarcoating.

Call it self-preservation—or even a coping mechanism, if you like—but I had learned over my lifetime that expectations are premeditated disappointments. It's better to be happily surprised than gravely disappointed. I can't imagine the crisis of faith I might have if God chose *not* to answer my prayers according to "*My* will being done." Don't get me wrong. I believe that God is a big and faithful God. However, I also believe that putting my hope in happy endings means putting my hope in hope itself rather than in the One in whom my hope is found.

More than anything, perhaps, I found attempts to infuse hope more than frustrating. I began to term other's comments "Happy Hope Band-Aids." They sounded like this: "Everything is going to turn out just fine. You'll see!" "Ben is going to survive this! I have a good feeling about it!" "You all have such a strong faith. No doubt God will honor that." "How could God not heal Ben with so many people all around the world praying for him?" I was often encouraged to "stay positive."

Little did these people know how positive I was staying! I was positive that God was *able*; I simply didn't know if He was *willing* to heal Ben. And I was absolutely positive that His glory was the main purpose of our journey…however it unfolded.

At every turn, we were reminded that Ben's leukemia was high risk and, in the words of Ben's primary oncologist, "This is a very bad disease you have, Ben." Perhaps against popular opinion, this particular doctor's approach was what we liked so much about him. There was no second-guessing him. He told things like they were. Funny enough, his initials were "A. X." and suitably he was affectionately called "Axe" by some of his colleagues. While he never minimized the severity of Ben's deadly disease, he never discouraged us in our pursuit to do all we could to remain positive. As a result, we took on a family motto that said, "Hope for the best, but prepare for the worst."

• • •

PRAYER JOURNAL ENTRY
Friday, September 19, 2008
Lord, it has come to our attention that there are some who think we're being "pessimistic" in our "realistic" approach to this whole scenario. It's becoming evident that some feel I am looking at the cup as half empty rather than half full. Both David and I agree that neither of us is hopeless or despairing. We definitely believe Your hand is in this and that You, the God of the impossible, can perform a miracle at any given moment.

God, give me the strength to accept Your will, whatever that will be. Of course, I hope that it includes healing Ben, but there are certainly no guarantees, no matter how heartfelt and faith-filled our prayers are.

The Ben Ripple

Father, draw Ben to Yourself. Hold him close and teach him Your ways. He is staying positive too, but we know that it takes more than a positive attitude to conquer life. His spiritual health is more important than his physical health. Speak to him through Your Word. He's strong, but his strength is bound to run out unless he draws on Yours.

Lifeline

"Find rest, O my soul, in God alone; my hope comes from him. He alone is my rock and my salvation; he is my fortress, I will not be shaken. My salvation and my honor depend on God; he is my mighty rock, my refuge. Trust in him at all times, O people; pour out your hearts to him, for God is our refuge" (Psalm 62:5–8).

• • •

Without question, it was a challenge to lead a private life in public. However, there were countless bonuses that far outweighed the frustrations.

It's hard to describe the feeling of lying helplessly on a stretcher and being carried to Jesus by the hundreds that were praying faithfully for us every hour of every day. It was a humbling experience, to say the least. We were absolutely overwhelmed by so many who rallied around our family to support us, not only prayerfully, but also very practically. Just when I thought they had exhausted the list of creative ways to help, they came up with something new to love us through the challenging time we faced!

• • •

PRAYER JOURNAL ENTRY
Tuesday, September 30, 2008
Where does the time go?

It's hard to imagine that we're now into our second month of Ben's leukemia. I continue to catch my heart choking every now and then. Tears well up at their leisure. Time still flies and life goes on, but with all the activity of the weekend I realize how much my life has gone into slow motion. What used to be normal life, with its normal activity at its normal pace, is now extremely overwhelming.

Taking one day, one minute, at a time certainly slows things down. Priorities become clear. Celebrations become more enjoyable. God's presence is that much more real.

Every now and then, I think about the process we began only forty-nine days ago. Shock, grief, loss of control, surrealism… these are life-defining words right now.

Sometimes I feel like I'm handling things so well that I wonder if I'm really handling it or if I'm just not really handling it at all. Maybe that's the truth right there, that I'm *not* handling it at all… *You* are, along with the others You've asked to carry us or carry the grief and burden.

When I asked Ben the other day how he's handling it, his reply was "I don't really think about it." Maybe that's where I am most of the time as well. We're simply living it and are too busy to take time to think about it.

We know that You're in control and understand that Your ways and thoughts are higher than ours and that You make all things beautiful in Your time.

Lord, am I due to crash eventually? Is there something lurking in the shadows that is going to test my faith to the max? An additional crisis?

People keep asking how we're handling things and marveling at our strength. The obvious answer is that Your strength is holding us up.

Lifeline

"I have posted watchmen on your walls, O [Lisa]" (Isaiah 62:6).

• • •

The next part of Ben's treatment made me extremely anxious. It required that he undergo ten consecutive radiation treatments to his entire brain! The reason for this was understandable; they needed to make sure that there was no leukemia hiding in his central nervous system. However, what wasn't so easy to digest was the fact that Ben's intelligent, witty, keen, and alert brain would now run the risk of slowness, memory loss, and "never-the-sameness." The whole situation caused me to lie awake at night.

I was invited to watch while technicians fitted Ben for his radiation mask. What began as a hard piece of screen-like plastic was immersed in a pool of water to soften it up before being stretched over and form-fitted to his entire face as he lay flat on his back and the mask was fastened to the surface beneath him. Two technicians worked together diligently and efficiently as they taped and lined things up. Even so, it seemed to go on endlessly. I found myself holding my breath as I imagined myself inside the mask that bolted my son to a table.

One of the technicians, Abby, sensed my need for reassurance and called me to her side to check on Ben.

I gently laid my hand on his and asked, "Ben, are you all right in there?"

He was unable to give me anything more than a "Mmhmm."

Then I was quickly escorted outside the room and directed to a waiting area while the treatment took place. I sat sobbing for the next five minutes of what again felt like an eternity. I was such a mess that even passersby took pity on me and offered me Kleenex.

Lost in my tears, I didn't notice Abby approaching me, having finished the treatment. Upon seeing my soggy state, she wrapped me in an embrace and said, "You don't have to be strong here."

I can't begin to describe the validation and freedom that simple statement gave me. Then she assured me that whenever she treated someone's child, she pictured her own lying there. Her empathy warmed my soul as she gave me permission to grieve yet one more huge loss.

· · ·

Prayer for Benjamin Elliott
Thursday, October 2, 2008

Ben was *great* through his entire half-hour procedure of measurements, radiation, etc., in a room that reminded me of a scene from *Star Wars*. He actually said it was quite relaxing! Wish I could say the same. Definitely hard on a mother's heart! Day one down!

We'll hopefully be hearing if one of us is a match in the next week or so.

From God's waiting room,

Lisa (Mom)

Prayer for Benjamin Elliott
Tuesday, October 7, 2008

Ben's radiation treatments will be half over tomorrow, and we're praising God that to this point they have been uneventful. His initial headaches and nausea, due to the radiation, have been taken care of with yet another bottle of pills.

Just this morning, we were notified that two of Ben's hematologists would like to meet with us tomorrow while we're at the hospital for Ben's fifth radiation treatment. No doubt it is concerning our next course of action in one way or another.

My mind would love to run into the land of "what ifs" and down trails of anxiety and fears that may not even be a part of the road ahead, so if you could all pray that God would pack an extra dose of His strength and peace for this next leg of the journey, this mother's heart would sure appreciate it.

Strength will rise as I wait upon the Lord…

From His waiting room,

Lisa (Mom)

Lifeline

"Do not be anxious about anything, but in everything, by prayer and petition, with thanksgiving, present your requests to God. And the peace of God, which transcends all understanding, will guard your hearts and your minds in Christ Jesus" (Philippians 4:6–7).

PRACTICAL TIPS

Practical Ways to Help Someone in a Crisis

Often people are *begging* to come alongside someone who is facing a crisis, but they might have no idea what to do. The key is to offer their help without being offended if their offer is turned down. It may just not be the right timing.

Here are some practical examples of the ways people sought to help us.

HOUSEHOLD HELPS:

Lawn care

Snow removal

Gardening

Housecleaning

Childcare

Housesitting

Preparing meals

PRACTICAL GIFTS:

Transportation

Gift cards

Freezable meals in disposable containers

Personal items (if you know of specifics that wouldn't embarrass
—deodorant, toothpaste, shower gel, shampoo, etc.)

Loan of a car

Hotel expenses

PAMPER ITEMS:

Candles

Magazines

Chocolate

Munchies

Microwave popcorn

CDs of inspirational or quiet music

Healthy snacks

Gift certificates for massage therapy, manicures, pedicures, and facials

Care packages

HELPFUL HINTS FOR MEAL PREPARATION:

Call ahead and let the person or family know your intention to bring a meal. Then ask, "Is that something you could use at this time?" If not, assure them you'll call again another time.

Ask if the person or anyone in the family has any food allergies or dislikes.

Ask if there are any family favorites.

Ask what they have had not enough of or too much of lately. (My family developed an allergy to lasagne!)

Send the meal in disposable containers or in a box or tote with instructions to leave all the food containers in it and put it outside the door for pickup. That way, they don't have to visit at the door unnecessarily, especially if it's not a good moment in time.

Label and provide cooking instructions. It's always good to know what you're about to eat and how it will taste most flavorful.

CHAPTER 3

THE *Perfect* MATCH

Being the strong-willed, determined person that he was, it took someone strong in her own right to rein Ben in. He had met his match in Sarah, who was bubbly, feisty, and independent, with a mind of her own.

Sarah loved Ben from the first day she laid eyes on him. Fortunately for her, she found her inroad when six years earlier Ben conveniently became best friends with her older brother, Josh. At that time, he was immediately unofficially adopted into their family.

On November 7, 2006, Sarah and Ben's mutual interest in one another was realized, and during the next two years of their dating relationship a romantic part of Ben came alive that none of us had ever witnessed. He put time, thought, and creativity into their dates. He expressed that the last thing he wanted was to waste their time together as couch potatoes. On special occasions such as her birthday, Christmas, or their dating anniversaries, he asked for my "female opinion" and feedback on gift suggestions.

For such a young couple, they had a mature love. They found a healthy balance and respect for each other's individuality by encouraging each other in friendships and activities outside of each other. There was no question that they loved being together. They shared interests, hopes, and dreams for their future together. But most importantly, they shared a mutual love for the Lord Jesus.

Throughout his illness, Sarah remained faithful to Ben. She visited as frequently as she could and dropped everything to be at his side when he needed her. Ben and Sarah wanted and needed to be together. We were sensitive to give them the time that Ben felt he was up to spending alone with her. She was one of the few people outside of our immediate family that he wanted to see, and we welcomed her visits.

She usually walked into Ben's room bouncing, smiling, and full of zest, with a bag full of things to occupy her in case he had to nap. Of course, napping was the last thing he wanted to do with her there. He wanted to take in every minute they had together. He was genuinely interested in hearing her chatter endlessly about life beyond the hospital walls. She kept his mind alive and active. She laughed at his dry sense of humor and lovingly tolerated his irritability on days when his illness got the better of him, as infrequently as he let on to her. She stroked his ego and encouraged him when he needed a boost. It was obvious that she loved him—in sickness and in health.

Sarah was no doubt Ben's one and only love—his perfect match! Who knew that he would one day be looking for another perfect match via an international bone marrow registry?

• • •

Prayer for Benjamin Elliott
Tuesday, October 7, 2008
The news has just come that we have no related match for Ben's bone marrow. We are getting through this difficult moment and will still meet with the doctors tomorrow to chart the next step of our course in search for an unrelated match.

God is still in control, even as I remind myself to breathe.

Lisa (Mom)

PRAYER JOURNAL ENTRY
Wednesday, October 8, 2008
We found out yesterday that we have no related match for Ben. Ugh! There are no words to describe how I am feeling. Disappointed? Yes, but my tears are more induced by the shock. The finality. The "what now?" as we head into more unknown territory.

We'll now be looking for an international match, which is not as ideal.

Lord, You're the Creator who so fearfully, wonderfully, and uniquely created each of us. You alone know if there's someone out there who'll be able to donate life to Ben. You are the giver and sustainer of life. You've numbered each of our days before there was one of them.

We'll be meeting with two of the doctors on Ben's hematology oncology team to discuss the road ahead. Lord, You have gone before us this far, so lead us in the way everlasting. Give us strength to face each step along the way.

Prayer for Benjamin Elliott
Wednesday, October 8, 2008

We just got back from London a while ago with moods suiting the rainy weather. Ben is handling things very true to himself and continues to take things in stride, so I'll consider my tears as my gift to him.

Unfortunately, there's no news other than timelines as we move into yet another waiting room, waiting eight to ten weeks for blood work, which is being shipped to Princess Margaret Hospital in Toronto to find an unrelated match. Then three more months minimum of waiting for an actual transplant in the case that a match is found, and in the case that Ben is even approved to have it performed as they weigh the risks of transplant versus carrying on with the treatment plan.

I was trying to put a word to my feelings just now. David used the word "disappointed," and so did Erin, as she was truly expecting to be Ben's match. (As it turns out, Natalie and Erin are perfect matches with each other.) As for me, I'd say I am disheartened. Any way you term it, we all simply hoped there would be a match amongst our family, and hope has been deferred. So my heart is sad. Terribly sad.

Learning to trust while we wait,
Lisa (Mom)

PRAYER JOURNAL ENTRY
Thursday, October 9, 2008

Today was a very interesting drive to the cancer clinic. It's one that I'm sure I'll remember for the rest of my days.

Ben opted not to plug his iPod in. This was my first clue that there was something on his mind. Typically he plugs it in and tunes me out as we drive the hour to get to the clinic.

As we drove, he finally broke the silence with "Mom, let's say that I'm gone in a year." Gulp! No doubt sensing that I was suddenly working hard to keep the car on the road, he continued, "I'm not saying that I'm going to be. The reason that I wouldn't be is that I don't feel that I've accomplished God's purpose for my life yet."

Fighting the tears that threatened to blind my driver's vision, I painstakingly responded with "Well, Ben, I don't think you realize just how much purpose you are already fulfilling as we speak. There are already hundreds around the world who are being inspired and impacted for God's glory as they join our journey of faith. At the same time, I don't know that any one of us has just one purpose to fulfill in life. Rather, I believe that we can choose to live purposefully each and every day of our lives. In fact, you can begin today!"

I could tell he was meditating deeply on my words. As they penetrated, I could see his gears churning.

"I think I'll register for my online chemistry course," he said. "And maybe I'll take some piano lessons. I've also been thinking a lot about how cool it would be to lead some youth Bible studies over the webcam!"

We carried on to the clinic in a whole new frame of mind.

• • •

From this day on, it became obvious that Ben was striving to give it his best shot to live purposefully, starting right then and there!

• • •

Prayer Journal Entry
Monday, October 13, 2008
I've been claiming Psalm 139 every day this week, since Tuesday's news of no match for Ben. On Wednesday morning, I woke up to Jacob strumming a song by Tommy Walker, "He Knows My Name." At Thursday evening's worship practice, I walked into the church as the worship team was singing the same song. Then we sang it again on Sunday morning—or at least everyone around me sang it as I stood and wept.

You know every chromosome and gene in Ben's body, Lord. You created him. You know if there's a match or not. You know the route we're taking. You've checked out all the avenues and bends in the road. You know when the road will get steep.

I'm trusting in You, Jesus, to lead us and pave the way. I don't have to worry about the road ahead. I just have to follow Your lead, taking one step at a time and trusting You.

Prayer for Benjamin Elliott
Tuesday, October 14, 2008

With the recent news that we have no related match for Ben's bone marrow, it's been a very emotional week. God continues to give us strength for each day, and we are so grateful.

There is no question in our minds that our God is able to find a perfect match from the over eleven million donors on the registry; there's always room for one more! But we also have to prepare ourselves in case He has another plan in store and there isn't a match. Isaiah 55:8 reminds me that His thoughts are not our thoughts, nor are His ways our ways.

God continues to remind me how little control we have, while at the same time how interested He is in the intricate details of our lives. A song that conveys this truth so clearly, and one that has been on my heart all week long, is "He Knows My Name," by Tommy Walker, based on Psalm 139. Amazingly enough, we ended up singing it at church this Sunday morning. I'm claiming this psalm for Ben.

I believe with all of my heart that all we are going through as a family is about bringing glory to the God who knows and cares about each one of us and who is able to do immeasurably more than we ask or imagine. The tough part is letting God be God and not interfering in His plan when things don't seem to go the way we *think* they should. I am learning to trust Him on a whole new level.

As we head down this unknown path, we are assured that God will be our guide. We are also so thankful for all of you who have chosen to journey along this road with us.

From His waiting room,
Lisa (Mom)

Lifeline

"O Lord, you have searched me and you know me. You know when I sit and when I rise; you perceive my thoughts from afar. You discern my going out and my lying down; you are familiar with all my ways. Before a word is on my tongue you know it completely, O Lord. You hem me in—behind and before; you have laid your hand upon me. Such knowledge is too wonderful for me, too lofty for me to attain. Where can I go from your Spirit? Where can I flee from your presence? If I go up to the heavens, you are there; if I make my bed in the depths, you are there. If I rise on the wings of the dawn, if I settle on the far side of the sea, even there your hand will guide me, your right hand will hold me fast. If I say, 'Surely the darkness will hide me and the light become night around me,' even the darkness will not be dark to you; the night will shine like the day, for darkness is as light to you. For you created my inmost being; you knit me together in my mother's womb. I praise you because I am fearfully and wonderfully made; your works are wonderful, I know that full well. My frame was not hidden from you when I was made in the secret place. When I was woven together in the depths of the earth, your eyes saw my unformed body. All the days ordained for me were written in your book before one of them came to be. How precious to me are your thoughts, O God! How vast is the sum of them! Were I to count them, they would outnumber the grains of sand. When I awake, I am still with you. If only you would slay the wicked, O God! Away from me, you bloodthirsty men! They speak of you with evil intent; your adversaries misuse your name. Do I not hate those who hate you, O Lord, and abhor those who rise up against you? I have nothing but hatred for them; I count them my enemies. Search me, O God, and know my heart; test me and know my anxious thoughts. See if there is any offensive way in me, and lead me in the way everlasting." (Psalm 139:1–24).

Prayer for Benjamin Elliott
Thursday, October 16, 2008
Radiation is complete! In Ben's words, "Hallelujah!"
Thank you as always for keeping us in your thoughts and prayers.
Lisa (Mom)

Prayer Journal Entry
Thursday, October 16, 2008
In light of the everyday drives to and from London and all the family activity, including concerns over Ben's condition, I haven't had the time I've needed to

be alone with You, Lord. So I'm trying to put into practice what I'm speaking on this weekend: "Fanning the Fire Within," taking time to be still and waiting in Your presence while You recharge me. Renew my strength, transform my weariness, and grant me patience.

I'm reminded, yet again, to come away to a quiet place to meet with You.

Lifeline

"Do you not know? Have you not heard? The Lord is the everlasting God, the Creator of the ends of the earth. He will not grow tired or weary, and his understanding no one can fathom. He gives strength to the weary and increases the power of the weak. Even youths grow tired and weary, and young men stumble and fall; but those who hope in the Lord will renew their strength. They will soar on wings like eagles; they will run and not grow weary, they will walk and not be faint" (Isaiah 40:28–31).

• • •

While we began our search for an international bone marrow match, Ben's illness made international news. God began showing up in unexpected ways. It wasn't unusual to have an email or Facebook message begin with "Hi. You don't know me but…" People went on to tell me how much our journey was touching their lives. The local newspaper also continued to take great interest in our story, which stirred up even more community interest. At this point in our journey, I realized that the things that were playing out in our life were much bigger than we were likely aware.

A few weeks after the first newspaper article was put to print, we were contacted by the reporter who put the article together. He wanted permission to pass on our contact information to a family in South Carolina. It had something to do with T-shirts?

I sat beside David as he made the call to a family who lived there, wondering at the tears rolling down his cheeks as he listened to another father's heartbreaking story.

I allowed my husband's words to fill the page of my next update.

• • •

The Ben Ripple

Prayer for Benjamin Elliott
Tuesday, October 21, 2008

Just yesterday, a UPS driver delivered thirty-six T-shirts from South Carolina. They had been sent by a couple who, just four weeks earlier, had buried their youngest of four sons, Ben. Ben was only twenty-six years old when he lost his two-year battle with cancer.

On Thanksgiving Monday, I had the humbling privilege of speaking with Ben's dad, Dan, who told me Ben's story. He spoke about visits to emergency rooms, surgeries, treatments, and how he and his wife, Linda, had cared for their dying boy at home for months until his heartbreaking death on September 9. I asked how he, all the way down in South Carolina, had heard about our Ben way up here in scenic Stratford.

Back in July, some of their family and friends decided to put on a fundraising concert. They called the special event "Ben-efit for Ben." As part of that event, they sold dozens of T-shirts emblazoned with the words "Believe for Ben. Let go—let God!"

After Ben's death in September, his father felt that the remaining unsold T-shirts should not be simply discarded or passed on to Goodwill. Instead, he sensed that they needed to be sent to someone somewhere… but he didn't know who or where, so he went to his computer and simply typed in the words "Ben Cancer."

The first hit was the story that our paper had run about our Ben in late September. He added that as soon as he saw that article, he knew that he had to send the T-shirts to us.

I asked my wife this simple question a few days ago: "Why is God sending us thirty-six T-shirts from South Carolina?" I can only call this a *divine intersection!*

What we've decided to do with the T-shirts is raise money for the Canadian Cancer Society.

Sharing God's glory to the ends of the earth,
David (Dad)

CHAPTER 4

Surviving
A FAMILY CRISIS

Seven months, thirty weeks, two hundred ten days. No matter which way you look at it, the next step on our journey was intense. It was aptly called "The Intensification Phase." This phase of treatment was divided into three-week cycles. Each cycle included daily oral chemotherapy of up to eighteen pills and weekly intramuscular chemo (hip needles), and every third week Ben would receive chemo intravenously. Then the cycle would begin all over again.

While there were days when I felt I was finally getting used to our new routine, there were some things I wasn't sure I ever would. For one, as handsome as Ben was and as unfazed as he was about being bald, it bothered me no end. The scar that marred his otherwise perfectly shaped head was a constant reminder of all his unsuccessful brain surgeries. It made me nauseous to look at the PICC line that extended out of his arm. It was also hard to look at his steroid-effected puffy face, pasty complexion, and bloated belly. Even so, it wasn't until I had the opportunity to see him through a friend's eyes one day that something occurred to me: *Ben looked like a cancer patient.*

It wasn't only his physical appearance that was changing, but also his physical ability. Every now and then he wrapped his hands around his thigh, poking fun at himself at how much muscle mass he had lost. Meanwhile, I cringed inside. Walking at a snail's pace alongside him as he shuffled to keep up with me was beyond heart-wrenching. It was especially hard whenever I pictured him only months before on the volleyball court or riding his bike. Exertion was getting difficult for him. *Everything* was getting difficult for him.

. . .

Prayer for Benjamin Elliott
Tuesday, October 28, 2008
Ben's feeling pretty lousy since his treatment last Wednesday. He's feeling tired, lethargic, and all-over yucky. He's got a headache today, along with a newly developed rash all over his upper body. Ben's symptoms are new every morning… but so are God's mercies!

God continues to give us daily strength and stamina to stand up to the daily tests. His mercies truly are new every morning. We're traveling this journey from strength to strength, not making many plans further down the road than an hour at a time.

Celebrating this moment as a gift from God,
Lisa (Mom)

Lifeline

"Because of the Lord's great love we are not consumed, for his compassions never fail. They are new every morning; great is your faithfulness. I say to myself, 'The Lord is my portion; therefore I will wait for him.' The Lord is good to those whose hope is in him, to the one who seeks him; it is good to wait quietly for the salvation of the Lord" (Lamentations 3:22–26).

. . .

The Intensification Phase wasn't intense for Ben only but also for David and me. It was definitely taking a toll on our marriage. Needless to say, there was bound to be some conflict. Oftentimes it was over the smallest of things. Fortunately, we had learned early in our relationship that we needed to accept our differences and use our conflicts to strengthen our relationship rather than divide it. Ministry, too, had taught us that life is too short to argue over which way to hang the toilet paper or where to squeeze the toothpaste.

Of course, we all know that toilet paper should be hung like a waterfall! And toothpaste should be squeezed from the end of the tube!

• • •

Prayer Journal Entry
Tuesday, November 4, 2008

David's always been good about easing and affirming my PMS state by saying that my overreaction to life is not that what I'm contending with is a non-reality, but rather that it's a magnification of reality. This is the way I'd describe life over the past few months. Perpetual PMS! It also explains a bit of my emotional state and some of the friction right now between David and me. We're dealing with so much reality. Given our mental and emotional state, we're prone to make issues larger than they would be under normal circumstances—like, tenfold!

I think it is an accumulation of many things, but mainly emotional exhaustion from dealing with lots of emotional weight on Ben's behalf. I don't always allow it to surface in my functioning mode. Also, I need to consider the mental and physical exhaustion in light of relentless ministry demands and facing fears of the unknown concerning Ben's bone marrow transplant, along with the stress of waiting for a donor.

As if these things aren't enough, there's the pressure of company coming and going, coordinating the activities of the other kids, keeping the house at a standard of cleanliness that will keep us all healthy—especially Ben—and we're both tired. We've been passing the car keys for weeks. We're emotionally spent, yet life keeps going on. It's hard to make plans, as each day holds some new event to control.

It's no wonder that our different responses cause sparks to fly every now and then, considering the stress we're both under. David's got a checklist for absolutely everything, and I'm so easily overwhelmed by it. I'm trying to pace myself in slow motion while feeling inflicted with his checklist. It doesn't help that we haven't been able to have regular time out together. Our dates consist of a ten-minute walk from the hospital to the hotel at the end of the day. I can't help but wonder what it will be like to sleep with him again. Maybe the question is, *will* we ever sleep together again with both of us on 24/7 nursing duty? I miss him.

I finally crashed last night at bedtime.

Lord, I'm tired. I need Your strength. I need Your perspective. I need Your inspiration. I don't think I can handle one more blow, Lord. But You know me and what I can handle better than I do. Lord, I commit this all to You. I trust in You.

• • •

I wasn't sure how much more this mother's heart could handle as I helplessly watched Ben suffer the physical, emotional, and social consequences of his disease. Everything inside me yearned to do something to alleviate the pain and discomfort that he was experiencing as I sat at his side each and every minute of each and every day.

• • •

Prayer Journal Entry
Sunday, November 16, 2008
This afternoon, David began watching a Sick Children's Hospital program dealing with childhood cancer. Not an especially good choice of programs for me to be watching right about now. However, I joined him for a few minutes.

Watching mothers holding and rocking their babies made me long to be able to hold, hug, and cuddle Ben when he's feeling so horrible. Another part of me is thankful that he's old enough that me just being around and available to meet his practical needs is sufficient.

Lord, I know You heard the longing of my heart, because as I eventually sat myself on the couch upstairs Ben joined me and laid his head on my lap, asking me if I would massage his head a bit. Thank You, Lord, for such an incredible gift via such a simple gesture. I love being his mom.

• • •

Life with a cancer patient was different than I expected, although I can't say I really knew what to expect. Now that I was on the inside looking out, it was more about learning that life still went on, even within our home. Bills still had to be paid, dishes and laundry still had to be done, and ministry life still demanded time and attention. And while Ben consumed much of my time and attention, I *did* have three other children who also needed me.

Natalie had been away at college for a year and had put her plans on hold to help manage life on the home front. This proved to be quite a challenge as family dynamics were forever changing, depending on if Ben was in the hospital or at home. Jacob was making the adjustment to not always having Ben to room or hang out with. Poor Erin didn't know if she was coming or going half the time.

This was a constant challenge to contend with. We had already spent Jacob's birthday in the hospital, squeezed Erin's in between treatments, and Natalie's was coming up one week before Christmas!

To anyone watching our lives, most days it would have appeared as much like a family *circus* as a family *crisis*. This was a tightrope walk like none other I'd experienced. It was hard to juggle all the balls at once. At times I felt as if I was the woman pinned up against a wall while knives are thrown, oftentimes seemingly blindfolded. Other times I felt like the lady lying in a box that is sawed in two. (On second thought, maybe that wasn't a bad idea! Oh, to have had two halves so that I could have more effectively ministered to the needs of my entire family at once!)

David and I knew that we weren't perfect, but we were doing the best we could. The biggest challenge was performing before a *live* audience!

• • •

Prayer for Benjamin Elliott
Sunday, November 16, 2008

Someone recently asked me, "So, what does a typical day in the Elliott household look like these days?" I would have to say in response that, although there's never a dull moment in light of Ben's condition, much of life is falling into a routine of sorts.

A typical day starts with getting everyone up and out the door for school and work while allowing Ben to rise slowly and begin his daily regimen of oral chemo and medications.

We have a daily visit from the VON nurses.

Naps are always in order, most of the time a couple per day, as sleep at night can be scarce.

By evening, Ben has the most energy he can muster up before once again heading to bed.

Of course, all of this is open to change by the hour depending on where Ben is in his treatment plan and what his reactions turn out to be.

We head to the hospital weekly for his treatment, which is always an all-day affair.

The odd day, if he's up to it, Ben will join David or me for a local excursion, usually remaining in the car. As of late, he's been able to attend a few of his high school volleyball team's tournaments.

We're planning life no farther ahead than an hour at a time. Anything outside of that gets too overwhelming. It keeps us living life in the moment, which I'm finding is still the safest and most manageable place to live.

Every now and then I'm reminded of the emotional weight of this "new normal," necessitating a good teary release. What an assurance it is to know that the God who leads us along this unknown road totally *gets* my fears and pain! As Ben would say, "He just gets it, folks!"

In reading God's "love letter" to me today, He drew my attention to Psalm 46:10—*"Be still, and know that I am God; I will be exalted among the nations, I will be exalted in the earth."* It's my comfort and prayer that as we still ourselves before Him, resting in His sovereignty, God's glory will extend to the nations.

We appreciate your continued prayers and practical expressions of love and concern.

Wrapped in His arms of love,

Lisa (Mom)

• • •

Years ago, David and I had the privilege of taking a trip to the Holy Land. Loaded with cameras, each of us on the tour was told that we had the freedom to take as many pictures as we wanted. However, we were also told that the most impactful pictures would be the ones we took with our hearts, things that were bound to leave a lifelong impact. I called these "Kodak moments of the heart."

As I watched Ben battle for his life, I often thought of Mary, the mother of Jesus, as she watched her own son battle through life, then ultimately suffer and die. She learned quickly to treasure these things in her heart (see Luke 2:19).

You can be sure that I took many snapshots and treasured each one. I took pictures of simple things, like:

Watching Ben enjoy his food when he was able to eat.

Watching him breathe easily in sleep.

Walking outside together and chatting on the park benches in the hospital gardens while we fed the birds.

Touring the hospital after hours in his wheelchair.

Seeing him walk down the hospital hallway without a walker.

Laughing at his hospital humor.

Taking note of his interactions with hospital staff and the obvious effect he was having on them.

Relishing the times when our entire family was able to sit around the dinner table at home.

I also took some painful pictures. For instance, Ben sitting at the sidelines of his high school gym, watching his volleyball team play the games he had been meant to captain. It was difficult to think about the active life he should have been living. It was excruciating to realize that in a very literal sense his life was passing him by while he sat on the sidelines.

Maybe one of the most bittersweet Kodak moments came when we attended Ben's high school commencement. People had been praying for this special occasion for months, as we knew what a significant event this would be in Ben's life and how important it was to him that he be a part of it.

It became painfully obvious that life was moving on without Ben… right before our very eyes. It was painful beyond description. While friends of his were commencing the next phase of their lives, Ben was commencing yet another phase of his treatment.

• • •

Prayer for Benjamin Elliott
Friday, November 28, 2008
Ben was discharged last Sunday, a day earlier than originally planned, which was a nice surprise. His headache was still in full swing and has persisted even to this day, but after discovering that there was no CNS (central nervous system) involvement of the leukemia, the oncology team wasn't concerned.

He's really hoping to get to his high school commencement tonight, as long as he's up to it. Since Wednesday, he hasn't been able to sit upright, so sitting up for even an hour will be a challenge, not to mention walking across the platform.

As much as we're always happy to be home, Ben voiced that he misses the comforts of our hospital home. I must agree that there is a certain feeling of security there for all of us, as nursing care is just the push of a button away.

I apologize if this update hasn't been as upbeat as others. We are not discouraged; nor have we lost hope. We are, for the most part, keeping our heads above water. The water just seems a little deeper lately, and it's harder to tread when you're tired.

Thankful also for all of you who are helping to keep us afloat!
Lisa (Mom)

Lifeline

> "When you pass through the waters, I will be with you;
> and when you pass through the rivers, they will not sweep
> over you" (Isaiah 43:2).

Prayer for Benjamin Elliott
Saturday, November 29, 2008

You'll have to bear with this particular update, as it's a Kodak moment from a mother's heart.

Ben had orchestrated a bunch of his buddies from school going out for a pre-commencement dinner. We dropped him off at the restaurant around 5:00 p.m., and the deal was that we'd pick him up again at 6:00, knowing that was about all he'd be able to handle. After his dinner, he walked into the house, stripped down, lay down, and finally threw up just as we were preparing to leave for the ceremony.

Once he was done, he said, in Ben-like fashion, "Well, that feels better... let's go, or we'll be late!" So out the door we went—just Ben, David, and me. Our next feat was to see if he could make it through the ceremony.

I had a meltdown as he marched up the aisle along with all the other graduates, amazed that he was even keeping up with them, as he hasn't walked farther than thirty yards for a few weeks or at a pace any faster than a stabilizing step-by-step effort.

The night was pretty uneventful, just like any other commencement ceremony I've ever been to. There wasn't any applause for individuals until each group of students had received their scholarship or award... that is, until Ben's name was called. Then the entire crowd broke out in what seemed like endless applause and cheering, with whistling and hoots and hollers. It made me proud. It made me feel like we'd won yet another small victory. But it also made me sad, as it naturally allowed me a moment to ponder all the aspects of his life that should have been.

All in all, I think we're handling this turn of events pretty well. It just gets emotional at times like this.

Treasuring these things in my heart,
Lisa (Mom)

PRACTICAL TIPS

Helping Your Children Through a Family Crisis

Any parent dealing with a crisis involving more than one child faces the challenge of giving each child the attention he or she needs. The following are suggestions for making sure each child feels loved and validated.

- Make yourself readily available any time, day or night.
- Don't put them on the spot as you inquire about how they're doing.
- Begin a family journal.
- Let them express their feelings without analysis, judgment, or criticism.
- Have family checkups.
- Express your personal feelings. Don't hide your emotions, or they may feel it's wrong or inappropriate to express their own.
- Take regular time alone with each child.
- Celebrate their personal victories, events, and special occasions with them.
- Be honest about what's going on (at the appropriate level of their understanding).
- Ask key questions:
- When do you think about _____ the most?
- What kinds of things trigger your thoughts/emotions?
- How are the kids at school treating you?
- Is there anything I can relay to your teachers/employer?
- Do you need some time off school/work?
- Are you feeling overwhelmed by school, work, friends, activity, etc.? How can I help alleviate some of that?
- How would you describe the way you're feeling in a word?
- Be sensitive to their surroundings. Don't ask them how they're doing in a crowd of their friends.
- Be sensitive to the time of day you choose to open doors of communication.
- Find ways to acknowledge the situation.

PRACTICAL TIPS (con't.)

- Follow their lead where communication and opportunity for connection is concerned.
- Remember that each child responds differently according to his or her personality and his or her way of processing.
- Respect their personal space.
- Initiate special times together where casual conversation can happen. For example, a shopping day, a shared event, or a family vacation.
- Watch for changes in or abnormal behavior patterns:
- Eating habits (not enough/too much).
- Changing friends.
- Tired all the time.
- Trouble socially or academically.
- Too much time alone.
- Withdrawal.
- Nightmares.
- Sleeping habits (not enough/too much).

CHAPTER 5

Christ "MESS"

The Christmas season was upon us. As we all know, Christmas can be a stressful time for anyone at the best of times. Stress is certainly something we didn't need any more of, especially during the worst of times! So we were determined to do all we could to make this as special a season as possible, however we could.

I began to count my blessings and enjoy all I could to help make our days be merry and bright in spite of the mess we found ourselves in. To begin with, I really enjoyed Ben's company, whether on our numerous travels to and from the cancer clinic or during the days spent alone at home together. I was always amazed, and even inspired, by how he could keep such a good attitude throughout all he was going through. It gave me reason to wonder how I would respond to something like that if *I* was the patient.

I was so thankful for my other three children and their grace and adaptability amidst all the comings and goings, changes and rearrangements.

I was especially thankful for the husband God gave me to travel this road with throughout all of its ups and downs and twists and turns. As Ben had said so well, "There's nothing we can do about it." So I strove to enjoy the ride.

We were also grateful to all those who surrounded us to bring glad tidings of comfort and joy, especially from some of the least expected sources.

• • •

Lifeline

> "Command those who are rich in this present world not to be arrogant nor to put their hope in wealth, which is so uncertain, but to put their hope in God, who richly provides us with everything for our enjoyment. Command them to do good, to be rich in good deeds, and to be generous and willing to share. In this way they will lay up treasures for themselves as a firm foundation for the coming age, so that they may take hold of the life that is truly life" (1 Timothy 6:17–19).

Prayer for Benjamin Elliott
Monday, December 8, 2008

For the past few months, a four-year-old member of our church, Lauren, has regularly been reminding her parents and brother that they need to be praying for Ben's "bows and arrows transplant." No wonder Jesus spent so much time with these precious ones! It does my own heart good.

She's also been sharing about Ben with her class at the Christian school here in town, prompting them to pray for Ben and our family.

Each member of her class sent an individual card to Ben to encourage him and make him aware of their prayers.

This morning, Ben was feeling well enough that he, along with David and I, ventured to the school to introduce himself to the class and thank them in person.

It was quite a moving experience as they first laid eyes on the recipient of their prayers. Each one introduced himself or herself, asked questions, and interacted with Ben as they enjoyed the treat he'd brought along for them. Then they took time to read him a group letter they had written together and individually signed.

Moments like these remind me of the innocence and faith of children. I'm grateful that the prayers of these precious babes in Christ are being laid at the feet of Jesus on our behalf. No doubt He listens to them and holds their faith near and dear to His own heart.

Deeply moved and blessed beyond words,
Lisa (Mom)

Prayer for Benjamin Elliott
Tuesday, December 9, 2008

As much of a blessing as our visit to the Christian school was yesterday morning, we're continuing to see the aftereffects that these little excursions have on Ben.

He was drugged up pretty good for his visit, and at times we could tell he was struggling for coherency.

He slept the remainder of the day, but even with our attempts to discourage him, Ben's determination won out, driving him to get out the door again last night for an important church business meeting he insisted on attending—to support his dad as much as anything.

Although we made sure he knew we could leave at any moment, he chose to stick it out until the "moment of decision" (the reason he had come to the meeting in the first place). Then one of his more frequent visits to hug a toilet came upon him.

It's 11:30 right now on the morning after, and he's *just* gotten up, made it as far as one of our couches, barely able to swallow an anti-nausea pill. Such is the nature of our lives these past weeks as we continue to deal with this intense, relentless headache—not to mention the excruciating muscle aches and now more frequent bouts of nausea.

With Christmas quickly approaching, I was reminded today that, while shepherds long ago watched their flocks by night, I am grateful to be able to keep watch over my own flock here at home.

Lisa (Mom)

• • •

By the time Christmas came around, Ben had already spent half of his days in the hospital dealing with one complication after another. This included three weeks over Christmas and New Year's that he didn't even remember!

• • •

Prayer for Benjamin Elliott
Sunday, December 14, 2008

Since this past Monday, Ben's been quite lethargic. He continues to lose muscle mass, and, along with the chronic headache, he's complaining of chest

47

pain with very little exertion. I failed math, but when you put these symptoms together they equal nil activity, which isn't helping the cause and, in fact, gives cause for concern.

On top of all of this concern is the news we received this week that thus far (nine weeks into our wait) they have not found a bone marrow match. Of course, this is the only thing on Ben's Christmas wish list, so this doesn't do a whole lot to boost our spirits.

At a time of year when we promote joy, hope, and peace, I'm thankful that even when we are sad Jesus gives us a deep joy that isn't based on circumstances. I am thankful that our hope is in the Lord, not whether or not we receive all the items we write down on our personalized wish lists!

From a weary, weepy mother's heart that is taking note of Ben's determination and *not* losing its joy, hope, and peace,

Lisa (Mom)

Prayer for Benjamin Elliott
Wednesday, December 17, 2008
We took Ben to the local hospital with severe leg cramps last night. While in the emergency room, David and I noted that Ben's left lower leg and ankle were significantly larger than his right. With the headache that Ben's been experiencing, a pain in his left calf has been of secondary concern for the past month or so. After having an ultrasound today, it has been confirmed that the pain Ben's been experiencing in his left calf is a blood clot. This will require a daily injection of a blood thinner for the next six months.

Thank you for your continued prayers, which in the most literal sense keep him through the night. I will update you with more details when I get them.

Lisa (Mom)

Prayer for Benjamin Elliott
Saturday, December 20, 2008
On the fifth day of Christmas, my good Lord gave to me...*a bone marrow match!*

Ben was rushed to the local hospital again yesterday morning. In the midst of everything that could go wrong, we got news of a bone marrow match for Ben! That's all we know right now, but we are so thankful for God's faithfulness and His provision in finding a potential donor. Ben's Christmas wish list is complete!

I am praising God despite the storm that continues to rage outside.

Lisa (Mom)

PRAYER JOURNAL ENTRY
Tuesday, December 23, 2008
Psalm 55:1–2 says, *"Give ear to my prayer, O God; And do not hide Yourself from my supplication. Give heed to me and answer me; I am restless in my complaint and am surely distracted"* (NASB).

This verse summarizes where I'm at right now—restless in my complaining. I don't feel there are any definite answers.

We are, indeed, surely distracted by so many opinions of so many people outside of the hospital walls—some contradicting, some flippant, some non-chalant, some arrogant, some distant, and some too hopeful. Some people offer answers to questions we're not asking, opinions they should keep to themselves, and questions we have no answers for. Others are simply frustrating.

I'm thankful for those who simply listen and have nothing to say.

Prayer for Benjamin Elliott
Sunday, December 28, 2008
'Twas the day before Christmas and all through the house, all were scurrying to get ready to head back to the hospital.

That's right. Ben was transported via patient transfer to the cancer care hospital early on Christmas Eve.

Home for Christmas? If only in our dreams! Ben was admitted on the spot in order to treat him and get another MRI of his head and spine to continue to make sure there were no cancerous cells.

I took up residency, watching over Ben's bedside by night and day, as David came down with a cold, disabling him from being able to even visit at the hospital let alone be Ben's roommate.

Later that day, we were able to get the other kids dashing through the snow with a little help from our friends, and they were able to spend the night at a nearby hotel in hopes that stockings would be hung by Ben's bedside with care.

The stockings were hung, but due to the prevailing sickness in the family, as well as the fact that Ben barely opened his eyes all of Christmas Day, we decided to give Jesus another birthday this year.

Please pray that God will move things along and perform another "Miracle on 34th Street."

As things are now, I've come home for the first time since December 24 to do some laundry and reacquaint myself with my house in preparation for when we can get Ben home so we can celebrate Christmas together as a family. Yes, presents remain under the tree, and now the stockings are hung again, but this time by the chimney with care in hopes that Ben Elliott soon will be here.

Skipping Christmas with the Kranks? Not this Elliott family! We'll be jingling all the way!

Looking forward to the homecoming,
Lisa (Mom)

Prayer Journal Entry
Saturday, January 3, 2009
A new year. A new day. A new life. Thank You, Lord, that Your mercies are new every morning. Thank You that your faithfulness prevails.

And so we begin this New Year in the middle of a storm in our lives that every now and then threatens to consume and overtake us. But, Father, I'm confident in You. I'm confident You have plans to give each of us hope and a future. I'm confident that You will receive the glory as a result of this journey You're taking us on.

Prayer Journal Entry
Sunday, January 4, 2009
Lord, I pray a date will become available very soon to meet with the transplant team so we can get on with the bone marrow transplant.

After surviving this past month of Ben being so sick and having the word "relapse" floating around in my brain, I feel You've used the experience to warm me up to the idea of a transplant. Going through a near-death transplant experience would be better than fearing the always-lurking relapse.

Prayer for Benjamin Elliott
Tuesday, January 6, 2009

We are praising the Lord today that we were able to get Ben home yesterday to finally celebrate our family Christmas... on the twelfth day *after* Christmas.

We are also praising Him that all of Ben's tests came back negative... which is actually positive! After more pokes, prods, and tests than he even remembers, it's been conclusive that Ben's still in remission!

His blood counts recovered significantly enough that the medical team performed his chemo treatment before we left. After packing up our accumulation of hospital-wear and equipment, we were on our way home.

Home... a word of perspective, I'm finding. It's rather amazing how "at home" we are in our little cubicle with our hospital family. They provide us with such a sense of stability and care extraordinaire! We are forever grateful for all who, in the most literal sense, helped us to survive Christmas.

So, as we venture into yet another year full of uncertainties and changes, we ask you to join us as we trust in the God who never changes. Pray that, while Ben remains in remission, he also regains his health and strength in order to be considered for the transplant.

We are so thankful for the many who have joined us on this journey of faith like no other we've journeyed before.

Trusting in the God who paves the way,
Lisa (Mom)

Lifeline

"I remember my affliction and my wandering, the bitterness and the gall. I well remember them, and my soul is downcast within me. Yet this I call to mind and therefore I have hope: Because of the Lord's great love we are not consumed, for his compassions never fail. They are new every morning; great is your faithfulness. I say to myself, 'The Lord is my portion; therefore I will wait for him.' The Lord is good to those whose hope is in him, to the one who seeks him; it is good to wait quietly for the salvation of the Lord" (Lamentations 3:19–26).

How to Come Alongside Someone Going Through a Crisis

Often it takes the wisdom of Solomon to know how to appropriately and sensitively come alongside someone in crisis. What do and don't you say? How can you help? Here's some sage advice along with practical ways to comfort others.

DO NOT THROW SURPRISE PARTIES (see Proverbs 27:14).
> Always call ahead. There are enough surprises when one is dealing with a crisis.

DO NOT SEND IN THE CLOWNS (see Proverbs 25:20).
> I don't always feel like laughing or being entertained.
>
> Don't help me look at the bright side… nothing seems bright, and nothing is normal. This only makes me feel guilty, that somehow feeling the way I do is wrong.
>
> Noise and high energy can be overwhelming to someone in pain or in crisis.

DO NOT GET "SLAP HAPPY" (see Proverbs 18:13).
> Quick fixes—like "Just get a good night's sleep!" or "Things will look better in the morning"— may not be accurate; nor are they always helpful. It's like applying a Band-Aid to a festering wound rather than applying salve to draw out the infection.
>
> Don't give me advice or answers to questions I'm not asking.
>
> Rather than helping me "get over" my crisis, "walk through" it with me.
>
> Don't lecture me by dictating how I should or shouldn't be feeling or where I should or shouldn't be in my state of being.
>
> Don't judge me for my raw emotion, language, or behavior.

┌─────────────── PRACTICAL TIPS (con't.) ───────────────┐

Do NOT ASK FOR DIRECTIONS (see Proverbs 25:14).

Offer specific help rather than saying "Let me know if I can do anything." I may not even know what I need, and my life is overwhelming enough without having to figure out what others can do to help me.

Make yourself readily available for when I do need company or assistance.

Do NOT MAKE ASSUMPTIONS (see Proverbs 19:2).

Don't assume that what you think I need is what I actually need.

Don't assume that because I'm not crying all the time that I'm "over" my pain or loss.

Don't expect a response to phone calls, emails, etc. It can get overwhelming.

Don't take charge without asking if I'd like you to. Sometimes I need to know I'm in control of something, and it can be overbearing when someone walks in and assumes responsibility.

Don't expect me to quickly resume life as usual.

└───┘

CHAPTER 6

A

Journey
OF FAITH

Bone marrow transplants aren't necessary for every patient with ALL (Acute Lymphoblastic Leukemia), but due to Ben's chromosome shift, making his a high-risk disease, he had to have one. During our hospital stay over Christmas, we often wheeled Ben around while he dreamed aloud of what food they might serve at the hospital where the transplant would take place. Food was the only thing he could think of enjoying, and even that was dictated by his chemotherapy, which left a thick residue on his tongue and the inside of his mouth that tainted everything he ate. Ben called it "chemo tongue." As we entered into the new year, our conversations took an exciting turn, especially when we discovered that there was not just one but four unrelated matches!

We talked about what life might look like once the transplant was over. There was a renewed sense of energy in the crisp winter air. Ben was excited about pursuing his career as a nurse, perhaps even a nurse practitioner in the hematology oncology field now that he had some experience behind him. He had already stored up a wealth of medical terminology and knew firsthand what nursing etiquette he preferred and how he might handle various nursing techniques. I asked him one day what he was looking forward to the most. He replied, "To live life again!"

Things were lining up perfectly, and it was evident that God was taking care of all the details to make the next leg of our journey of faith that much easier to bear.

. . .

Prayer for Benjamin Elliott
Wednesday, January 7, 2009

Every new year, I ask God to lay on my heart a verse or passage of Scripture that will be my focus throughout the coming year. This year was no exception.

Early on in this journey, I took hold of Psalm 40:1–10. Because God continues to draw me to it, I'm claiming this for this upcoming year. It says, *"I waited patiently for the Lord; he turned to me and heard my cry. He lifted me out of the slimy pit, out of the mud and mire; he set my feet on a rock and gave me a firm place to stand. He put a new song in my mouth, a hymn of praise to our God. Many will see and fear and put their trust in the Lord… I proclaim righteousness in the great assembly; I do not seal my lips, as you know, O Lord. I do not hide your righteousness in my heart; I speak of your faithfulness and salvation. I do not conceal your love and your truth from the great assembly"* (Psalm 40:1–3, 9–10).

I am a firm believer that nothing we experience in life is ever wasted. We can make our "mess" our "message." I believe that God allows us to go through various trials in order that somewhere down the road it may benefit someone else. It may be that there's even someone following these updates who is actually benefiting from my ramblings!

I am reminded every single day of this journey that this is *not* about *me!* Rather, it's about sharing God's glory so that others will see and know that there is a God who is interested in the most intricate details of their lives.

The fact is, God doesn't want me to seek comfort and normalcy, but rather He wants me to seek *Him!* I am learning to trust Him on a level I didn't think possible.

I have no control… and I'm good with it,

Lisa (Mom)

Prayer Journal Entry
Monday, January 12, 2009

Psalm 63:2 is perfect for describing where I'm at right now: *"I have seen you in the sanctuary and beheld your power and your glory."* Amen to that! I've been seeing Your glory time and time again since last August. Hearing how our journey is touching so many other lives, how it's changing peoples' perspectives and giving hope in their circumstances, moves me to tears every single time. It helps give me strength to take the next step.

Thursday, January 15, 2009

Something happened yesterday while we were at the clinic, something that struck both Ben and me. We were placed in a bed beside a woman dealing with her own cancer battle who had a friend accompanying her. We heard nothing but cursing and "attitude" ringing out the entire time we were there. Misery tried to find company with us when we were given opportunity to converse. Ben and I both commented after the encounter that she's going to find it quite challenging to fight this monster with the attitude she has, whining and complaining and expressing the inconvenience that this whole endeavor has caused her.

Aside from God's strength, I was reminded of what has made our own battle doable: Ben's attitude and his decision to roll with the punches. From the get-go, with a shrug of his shoulders, Ben's words have been "Nothin' much you can do about it." This has been the case whenever, with a lump in our throat or tears streaming down our cheeks, we've asked him how he feels about all the procedures, pokes and prods, and inconvenience this disease has caused him.

I woke up in a grump this morning. I'm tired. I'm experiencing a mixture of feelings lately ranging from anger to sadness to nothingness. I am enjoying my own company, solitude, quiet… in short, my own space. I guess it makes sense when I think of all the activity and emotional energy of the past few months. I haven't been getting much sleep since the hospital days, but that's no excuse! I know that I, too, have a choice to make—a decision to make it a good day. This is hard, because it's so easy to fall prey to ugliness, moping, and victimization. But what good does that do?

I've come to the conclusion that Ben is absolutely right! There's nothing any of us can do about our circumstances, but we can make the decision to be sure our attitude is right before God. We are given the choice to decide to respond to our situation in a manner that will honor and bring glory to God. We have the choice to make our lives count for something day by day, knowing that each day is truly in God's hands. Chuck Swindoll once said, "Life is twenty percent what happens to us and eighty percent how we deal with it."

Much of life happens to us… not by choice. I think Ben might be winning me over to his ways. I can choose to be like the woman we met at the clinic and fight, whine, and fall victim to it, or, like Ben, I can choose to go with, it knowing that there's nothin' much I can do about it.

Romans 8:28 says, *"And we know that in all things God works for the good of those who love him, who have been called according to his purpose."* Does this mean, as some believe, that bad things don't happen to good people? Au contraire. Rather, it is for our good that all things work to make us stronger, better people and also to transform us into His image (Romans 8:29), which is ultimately His purpose.

Lifeline

"Cast all your anxiety on him because he cares for you" (1 Peter 5:7).

PRAYER JOURNAL ENTRY
Saturday, January 24, 2009
As I walked today, enjoying the fresh air and sunshine, I felt a deep assurance that I'm where I need to be right now, and I'm grateful to have the privilege to enjoy it.

Recently, I was thinking about just how much of life we wish away when really there's so much we can enjoy no matter what's going on in our lives.

I'm enjoying the snow as an excuse to stay put. I'm enjoying my candles and hot tea. I'm enjoying my morning coffee. I'm enjoying dinnertime with everyone around the table. I'm enjoying making sure all the laundry is caught up and the meals are made. I'm enjoying my trips to and from the hospital with Ben. I'm enjoying meeting all the medical staff. I'm enjoying my fluffy ivory blanket that Erin got me last Christmas. I'm enjoying eating (maybe too much). I'm enjoying the sunshine, when it comes out. I'm enjoying my kids. It did my heart good to see Natalie, Jacob, and Erin all on the worship team last week. I'm enjoying watching birds at the feeder. I'm enjoying cleaning my house. All these simple pleasures bring joy to my heart.

Thank You, Lord.

Lifeline

"You hold me by my right hand. You guide me with your counsel… My flesh and my heart may fail, but God is the strength of my heart and my portion forever… But as for me, it is good to be near God. I have made the Sovereign Lord my refuge; I will tell of all your deeds" (Psalm 73:23–24, 26, 28).

Prayer for Benjamin Elliott
Friday, January 30, 2009

As you're all aware, we had our long-awaited meeting with the transplant team yesterday. I can hardly get my mind around all we were presented with, let alone try to wrap my heart around it.

Our appointment was three and a half hours, with only a half-hour break partway through when the doctors weren't with us. The team of eight doctors will make a decision on Monday as to whether or not to accept Ben for a bone marrow transplant. All indications from yesterday's visit were that Ben is a good candidate for the procedure... but we won't know for sure until Monday.

We found out yesterday that Ben actually has three matches, but none of them have been contacted yet. The team will discuss and decide which of the three matches will potentially be the best donor for Ben. That person will then be contacted and, if he or she agrees, will go through a rigorous medical assessment to make sure he or she is a healthy donor. This process usually takes somewhere between four to six weeks. If the potential donor passes all the medical requirements, he or she then becomes Ben's official donor. If he or she does not pass, the team proceeds with one of the other two potential donors.

Lisa (Mom)

Lifeline

"Blessed is the man who trusts in the Lord, whose confidence is in him. He will be like a tree planted by the water that sends out its roots by the stream. It does not fear when heat comes; its leaves are always green. It has no worries in a year of drought and never fails to bear fruit" (Jeremiah 17:7–8).

Prayer for Benjamin Elliott
Sunday, February 1, 2009

A memorable event from Ben's childhood was the day his junior kindergarten teacher came for a home visit. She asked him to sing one of his favorite songs. So, in usual Benjamin form, as he did with all our houseguests, he handed out the coloring and kids' books lying around. He then took his place behind the toddler table, a play microphone in hand, and told us to turn promptly to Hymn #39. Then he sang, loudly and clearly, "Holy, Holy, Holy... Lord God *on my team…"* (the actual words being "Lord God *Almighty*") I have never been able to sing this hymn the same since, and I now claim Ben's lyrics more than ever. Not only will Ben need his own determination and strong will, but he'll need the strength of the Lord God on his team.

The day after our visit with the transplant team was a pretty emotional one for me as the next "new reality" hit afresh. Once again, God in His perfect timing sent me a card via a friend who knows firsthand about what it is to celebrate "a new birthday," having been through a bone marrow transplant herself. 2 Corinthians 5:17 was written on the card: *"Therefore, if anyone is in Christ, he is a new creation; old things have passed away; behold, all things have become new"* (NKJV). She pointed out how a bone marrow transplant shows, better than anything, the wonderful transforming power of Jesus Christ in our lives as we are spiritually born again.

David, Ben, and I had the opportunity last night to process some of our fears and concerns about the days, months, and years to come—and, believe me, we were presented with enough of them. It was a sobering time.

With Ben's determination and strong will to lead us, along with God's strength, we build our resolve once more for this next leg of the journey. Thanking you as always for joining us,

Lisa (Mom)

• • •

As much as I was glad that we were all able to keep up a good attitude for the most part, there was no question in my mind that it would take more than that to get us through the next leg of our journey. It would most definitely take having the Lord God on our team. I don't know how others travel roads like this one without Him!

• • •

Lifeline

"Sing for joy to God our strength" (Psalm 81:1).

Prayer for Benjamin Elliott
Thursday, February 5, 2009
We just got word this evening that Ben has been approved for a bone marrow transplant. The next step is for the team to research which of the matches will

best suit Ben. That person will then be contacted to see whether or not he or she consents. Once he or she consents, a date will be set, and away we go.

Stay tuned…

Lisa (Mom)

• • •

There were many times throughout our journey that I could feel myself wandering into the land of "what ifs." Whenever I caught myself, I sensed God's word to my heart asking me, "Lisa, do you trust Me?" Each time, I had to step back and take inventory. Did I really trust Him? Did I trust Him with my children? Did I trust Him with my marriage? Did I trust Him in the day-to-day activities and minute-by-minute decisions? Did I trust Him with my future? Or maybe better yet, would I still trust Him when and if my faith was put to the ultimate test?

A memorable scene from the past often played out in my mind. Benjamin was only two years old. By this time, he had already grown out of his naptime, but with three young children I still desperately needed mine! Every day was pretty much the same battle. Once I got the other two kids settled, I put Ben into his room and gave him the option to either lie down or play quietly. That was successful for all of fifteen minutes before he began to creep down the stairs.

From the chair where I usually sat while the kids rested, I had a clear view of the stairway. Inevitably, I heard a muffled *thump, thump, thump*. I would turn to see my little blond-haired, blue-eyed Benjamin on his bottom, slowly making his way down the stairs. As he thumped along, he kept his eyes on me with a coy smirk that never ceased to charm me.

I'll never forget one time in particular. It was a cool winter's day, and I decided to make a fire. As I worked to build the fire, I felt a presence in the room. I turned to see Benjamin heading my way with a sheepish grin on his face. For whatever reason, I chose not to fight it that day but instead asked if he wanted to help me build the fire. He was thrilled!

As we worked together, out of the blue he began to relay the story of Abraham building an altar with a fire beneath it. "Just like this fire, eh, Mom?" he asked. He went on to fill me in on the rest of the story, including the fact that this was the place where God had asked Abraham to offer his promised son, Isaac, as a sacrifice. Then, after a strategic pause, he finished with the paradox that I had waited until Bible college to learn. He said, "That's kind of the same as God offering His only son, Jesus, on the cross to die for us, isn't it, Mom?"

With my mouth, I assured him, "Yes. That's exactly right, Benjamin." In my mind, however, I couldn't believe the insight of such a young boy. *My* little boy!

Who would have thought that less than twenty years after that significant conversation, I would be acting it out in my own life, daily offering my own son as a sacrifice to the God I loved?

· · ·

Lifeline

"Now faith is being sure of what we hope for and certain of what we do not see" (Hebrews 11:1).

PRAYER JOURNAL ENTRY
Thursday, February 19, 2009

A surreal feeling is settling in all over again. While it feels that this can't really be happening, each step brings us that much closer to the reality we face. I can't help but think that things are going to get much worse before they get better.

I can't help but think of Jesus in the Garden of Gethsemane, praying, *"My Father, if it is possible, may this cup be taken from me. Yet not as I will, but as you will"* (Matthew 26:39).

I don't like the reality we face. I don't want to drink from this cup, and yet, Lord, I know it's what You're calling me to do right now. You found a ram to replace Abraham's sacrifice of his son; I ask you to do the same for me.

Lifeline

"By faith Abraham, when God tested him, offered Isaac as a sacrifice. He who had received the promises was about to sacrifice his one and only son, even though God had said to him, 'It is through Isaac that your offspring will be reckoned.' Abraham reasoned that God could raise the dead, and figuratively speaking, he did receive Isaac back from death" (Hebrews 11:17–19).

· · ·

Family was always important to Ben, and having a wife and family of his own one day was his greatest dream. Therefore, it was no surprise that one of the dreams Ben began to discuss with me was related to Sarah. Whenever we had time alone, he would share some of his thoughts and feelings for Sarah. I came to find out that he had also been doing the same with his dad. In isolated conversations, he wanted to know what our thoughts were about Sarah.

He was interested in knowing how we felt about him asking her to marry him one day. He openly shared everything from how he might propose to his dreams for their future together. He spoke about their plans to live somewhere in the country and how excited he was about not only investing in, but also eventually designing, his own multipurpose riding lawn mower–snow blower. He shared creative thoughts as to how he would provide for their family. He even went as far as to design Sarah's wedding gown as he lay in his hospital bed. He drew house plans in a small notebook he kept at his bedside, allowing the nurses to give input when they caught him in action.

Therefore, I could almost physically feel Ben's pain the day he was told that once the bone marrow transplant took place, it was likely that he would never have children of his own. He was presented with the option of seeking out a fertility clinic if he so desired, but his chances of success were slim.

Regardless of the result, this step made sense to Ben in hopes that Sarah would bear *his* children one day. So we made all the necessary arrangements and, as always, hoped for the best while preparing for the worst.

Even so, nothing could have prepared me for the phone call I received the same day of our visit to the fertility clinic. We had been told to expect a call within a week, never expecting to hear back only a couple of hours later.

Ben and I were watching television when the phone rang. It was Jane-Ann, the kind and compassionate nurse at the fertility clinic. Her voice cracked with emotion. Through tears, she told me, "Likely due to the chemotherapy Ben has received, there was no viable sperm detected." My hopes were completely dashed. Another loss.

I hung up the phone, my heart in my throat, knowing that I now had to relay the message to Ben, who sat at my side in anticipation. After taking a deep breath, with tears welling in my eyes, I gave him the news. In a way that shouldn't have surprised me by this point, he looked me in the eye and simply asked, "When can I try again?"

• • •

The Ben Ripple

Prayer Journal Entry
Friday, February 13, 2009

Today we got the news that Ben will not be able to have children of his own. Although this was always a possibility, now it's a reality—and it hurts. This is what scares me as we face the reality of a bone marrow transplant: everything that can possibly go wrong becoming a reality. Help me, Lord, to *"go from strength to strength"* (Psalm 84:7).

Prayer for Benjamin Elliott
Monday, February 16, 2009

Ben is continuing to do really well. His headache is still relentless, and, although it is debilitating every morning, it is not to the point of making him nauseous, which he's really thankful for (as are the rest of us). His tummy's getting a little tough from his daily needles to treat his blood clot. Good thing he's tougher than tough!

He's been able to get out of the house and actually visit with a few friends in the past week, which has done him good. He's eating almost at full caliber again and is enjoying every mouthful! He's come up with a "fun things to do before the transplant" wish list, which we are aiming to fulfill. We are laughing together as a family a lot these days, living life to the fullest in all the ways we can. We truly have much to be thankful for!

I have to admit, it feels like the calm before the storm. And in fact, I know that it *is!* Each step we take in preparation for the inevitable storm ahead brings us more deeply into the reality of what exactly we're facing.

Yesterday I was able to get to church for the first time in months. I *knew* I was meant to be there. The words of the songs were meant for me! Then, through my husband's sermon, the Lord encouraged and challenged my heart from 2 Chronicles: *"'For we have no power to face this vast army that is attacking us. We do not know what to do, but our eyes are upon you.'... 'This is what the Lord says to you: "Do not be afraid or discouraged because of this vast army. For the battle is not yours, but God's... You will not have to fight this battle. Take up your positions; stand firm and see the deliverance the Lord will give you [Elliott family]. Do not be afraid; do not be discouraged. Go out to face them tomorrow, and the Lord will be with you"'"* (2 Chronicles 20:12, 15, 17).

God has not promised to remove the storm, but He *has* promised that He will be with us in the midst of it.

Standing firm, clinging to the Rock Who does not move in the midst of the storm,

Lisa (Mom)

Lifeline

"Be strong and take heart, all you who hope in the Lord"
(Psalm 31:24).

PRAYER JOURNAL ENTRY
Wednesday, February 25, 2009

Last night, David and I tried to figure out how to respond when people ask us how we're doing. It's a hard question to answer. Although we feel we're handling things as best as we can, functioning normally for the most part, the reality and heaviness of our crisis never quite goes away. I compare our lives to Ben's headache; there is always something there under the surface. Sometimes it's debilitating. Other times it allows us to function and do what we need to do. Various frustrations trigger intense emotions and thoughts about the severity of our situation, and usually when we least expect it. It would be nice to just take a pill to make it all go away!

Lifeline

"He who dwells in the shelter of the Most High will rest in the shadow of the Almighty. I will say of the Lord, 'He is my refuge and my fortress, my God, in whom I trust'… He will cover you with his feathers, and under his wings you will find refuge; his faithfulness will be your shield and rampart" (Psalm 91:1–2, 4).

• • •

Throughout my life, I have occasionally experienced what I call "holy nudges." I felt one of these nudges a month before the transplant was to take place, and it was to get Ben to see David's side of the family. Seeing as Ben wouldn't be going too far from home for the next long while after the transplant, I thought it was a good idea to take the opportunity to get him there ASAP. However, it was more than just a passing thought. It was an absolute drive inside of me to do whatever it took to get him there.

I knew that there was no possible way Ben could make the seven-hour trek by car in his condition, so I got the bright idea that he and his dad should book a flight. Ben would not only be thrilled to see his relatives, but he would be even more thrilled to board a plane!

David and I decided to invite Sarah and her parents along for the ride to the airport. That way, we could have a triple date to begin the adventure. We enjoyed a beautiful dinner at Ben's favorite Thai food restaurant, then dropped David and a very excited Ben off at the airport.

Inside the airport, Ben bought a bag full of penny candy. David described him like a kid in a candy shop—in the very literal sense. They took pictures boarding the plane and even got a video recording the takeoff and landing.

Ben got a kick out of surprising David's parents, and, although exhausted, when all was said and done, he was so happy to see many of his cousins, aunts, and uncles.

The entire plan couldn't have worked out any more perfectly. It was the trip of a lifetime in every way!

• • •

Prayer for Benjamin Elliott
Tuesday, March 3, 2009

As I write this update today, Ben and David are boarding a plane to come back home after a two-night stay in Ottawa! That's right, they boarded the plane on Sunday to go and surprise David's parents, who, due to circumstances in their own lives, aren't able to come see us. Being able to make the trip was one of the unwritten items on Ben's list. With his counts being stable, we felt the timing was right. It was good timing, as well, for the two of them to have some father-son time together.

Our journey right now feels as surreal as it did at its onset. Ben's hair is growing back, he's gradually gaining strength, and he's going on outings. He's as close to being his old self as he's been in six and a half months. We've fallen into as close to a routine as we possibly can, going through the motions of this new normal. It's when we have to administer his daily drugs, change his dressing, welcome the nurse into our home, or make our weekly trips to the cancer clinic that I'm kick-started back into reality.

I can't help but ask myself, "Is this really happening?" At these checkpoints, the motions turn into emotions. Tears are never far from the surface these days.

With a heart full of emotion as we go through the motions,

Lisa (Mom)

Prayer for Benjamin Elliott
Thursday, March 5, 2009

As you all know, we continue to wait for a date to be set for Ben's bone marrow transplant. I speak for myself when I say that things are a little bit edgy right now in light of this "precipice existence" we're living.

The deal is that we've got an apartment all lined up and leased for two months beginning mid-March, so it would be nice if Ben could be in the hospital during this course of time. I feel like I have to keep reminding God of this, when in fact I've just seen Him part the proverbial Red Sea to find us this apartment. In the words of the property manager, "We'll provide everything you'll need to make your stay comfortable so that you can focus on getting your son better."

There's hardly a time these days when I don't turn my head and see evidence that God is very much in this journey and is walking alongside us. In my head, I know that He will work everything out… as He has so many times over the past six and a half months.

Lisa (Mom)

Continuation of Thursday, March 5, 2009

So, just within the hour of having sent my previous update, I got a call… and you'll never guess from whom! You got it! It was the transplant coordinator calling to tell me that tentative dates have been set.

Oh, *me* of little faith,

Lisa (Mom)

Lifeline

"Trust in the Lord with all your heart and lean not on your own understanding; in all your ways acknowledge him, and he will make your paths straight" (Proverbs 3:5–6).

PRACTICAL TIPS ────

Caring for Yourself While You Care for Others

We were all doing our best to keep our heads above water, but it was becoming increasingly hard to tread. We were tired and worn down. One thing I had learned over the years is the importance of taking care of myself in order to care for others. I had spoken on this subject often, but now I was learning it all over again in a new way. Here are some ways I've found helpful:

- Allot time for pampering.
- Take regular timeouts for personal rest, rejuvenation, and stress relief—activities like gardening, cleaning, artwork, reading books, and taking nice relaxing baths or extra-long showers.
- Set healthy boundaries. Get to know your limitations. Learn to say "no."
- Make time for feeding on the Word of God. (Psalms are excellent in their honesty and authenticity.)
- Journal. Write down your thoughts, cares, concerns, joys, and sorrows. It isn't for everyone, but journaling can be very therapeutic.
- Try to get enough sleep at night or take a nap when you need one.
- Physical exercise is good for the body, mind, and soul. Try walks, runs, or workouts.
- Candles can easily create a mellow, restful atmosphere. (I personally like scented ones.)
- Soft or inspirational music can help dispel the spirit of heaviness, trading it in for the garment of praise.
- Drop expectations. We can be our own worst enemies, expecting more from ourselves than we ought.
- Eat properly. This isn't the time to be restricting yourself; however, it is important to eat wisely. Remember, everything in moderation.

PRACTICAL TIPS (con't.)

- Doing word or number games can divert your attention and don't require a lot of focus. They can easily be interrupted without causing frustration.
- Identify your support network, and exercise selective vulnerability. This means having a few people you can trust with your innermost emotions, frustrations, and ups and downs. These are the people who will keep you accountable and who will allow you to express your pain and raw emotions without judgment.
- Spend time with people and in activities that recharge and energize you.
- Massage therapy is something I wish I had tapped into much earlier than I did.
- Identify and grieve your losses. Losses don't occur only after the death of a loved one, but also during the illness.
- Build laughter into your life.
- Write standardized thank-you notes (instead of individualized ones) to save both time and energy. Both are things you may not have a lot of.
- Send mass emails to keep people updated with news, prayer requests, and praises.
- Assign one or two individuals as point people who can help relay messages and find the proper help to take care of personal and practical needs, meal coordination, family orchestration, and transportation.
- Find purpose in your pain by reaching into the lives of others as you're able. There is therapy to be found as we focus some of our attention beyond ourselves.

CHAPTER 7

Plan B

We were given a card in the early stages of our journey that read, "Life has a way of making quick turns without using a turn signal." This, of course, was becoming our motto! However, nothing could have prepared us for the news that blindsided us at a moment we were least expecting it.

Just two weeks before the transplant, the unthinkable happened. Ben's blood work revealed that he had relapsed. Not only did this mean Ben would be required to endure more painful injections into his spine to administer his chemo twice a week, along with another round of radiation to his entire spinal column, but this relapse significantly lessened his chances for survival.

For the second time on our journey, my world stood still… and this time I wasn't the only one to experience the stillness. There was a corporate hush as the thousands who had now joined our journey were shocked into silence. This didn't make any sense. God had paved the way so intricately, taking care of details that nobody could have put together outside of His handiwork and divine intervention. However, even then we had to trust that God had in mind a greater plan. I was about to learn that what I considered "Plan B" was always God's "Plan A."

• • •

The Ben Ripple

Prayer for Benjamin Elliott
Wednesday, March 11, 2009
We had a relatively uneventful day at the clinic today. In light of Ben's up-coming bone marrow transplant, chemotherapy was held off. However, in order to properly transition us into the hands of the transplant team, other medical procedures were performed. Up until this point all results have come back negative, for which we've been thankful.

Spirits were high. Nurses wished us well and hugs were given freely as we closed this chapter of the past seven months. Every patient who has completed their chemotherapy at the clinic has the privilege of ringing a bell on their last treatment day. Ben opted *not* to ring the bell today, as he felt that it wasn't really his final treatment.

Enter Plan B…

After we returned home, we received a call from our oncology team with news that, even as I write, has not yet fully sunk in. What do you do when your oncologist's first words are "I've got bad news"? Of course, bad news could have meant the inconvenience of having to reschedule some of the appointments I'd spent so much time preparing for. Never in a million years, however, was I expecting to hear that in today's tests, leukemia blasts had been detected, and the transplant therefore had to be cancelled. In other words, the cancer has progressed into Ben's central nervous system. In layman's terms, Ben has relapsed.

So, how is Ben taking this? His first words to me were "Well, obviously there's a reason for all of this." His next words were "It's a good thing I didn't ring the bell!"

Where does this leave us? *"We are hard pressed on every side, but not crushed; perplexed, but not in despair; persecuted, but not abandoned; struck down, but not destroyed"* (2 Corinthians 4:8–9).

Because Jesus lives, I can face tomorrow,
Lisa (Mom)

Prayer for Benjamin Elliott
Thursday, March 12, 2009
I hesitated to cancel the apartment that God had set up for us, feeling it was premature and that I should be getting a call any minute to renege. However, after receiving a number of phone calls this morning to cancel all the tests that were to take place over the coming couple of weeks, along with phone calls to

set up newly scheduled appointments, reality began to sink in. There's been *no* mistake.

I pray that we don't lose hope, that we will continue to cling to the Rock who does not move, that God will one day redeem for Ben the years the locusts have eaten, and that in turn God will receive all the glory. We don't know what the future holds, but we do know *Who* holds the future.

Lisa (Mom)

Prayer for Benjamin Elliott
Friday, March 13, 2009

I'm not quite sure how to articulate the whirlwind of emotions and thoughts that have taken place in my heart over the past forty-eight hours since receiving news of Ben's relapse.

Then again, from the responses I've received from so many of you, I don't think I have to, as it seems that we're all in the boat together, experiencing everything from initial shock to numbness, shuffled wanderings, long stares, confusion, deep heavy sighs, and many tears. Then the surreal feeling takes over. You wonder if somehow there's been a mistake; the results were misread. Then we begin asking, "Why this? Why now?"

I know some of you are angry, maybe even at God Himself for allowing this to happen. Please don't be; He's still in control. Plan B is not an interruption of our Plan A; it was His plan all along! It's not the storm we saw on the horizon initially, but God is still able to calm it!

Lisa (Mom)

Prayer for Benjamin Elliott
Saturday, March 14, 2009

This morning, Ben has woken up with an excruciating headache, causing pain and nausea.

Ben's headache may just match the heartache that I felt when I awoke this morning. Yesterday, by God's grace, David and I were able to move beyond the paralysis that we experienced upon news of Ben's relapse. Today is another story. I woke up with a heavy heart, and I've already shed many tears.

The only thing I can think today is that this twist in the road is a test of our faith.

The Ben Ripple

It occurred to me this morning when I went for my power walk with the Lord that this trial is one of God's ways of making sure both David and I are truly practicing what we're preaching in both our lives and ministry. It is no mistake that David is preaching about finding joy amidst life's circumstances, and I've recently been working on speaking material for an engagement I have in June titled "Living Life in the Moment" (about living the abundant life no matter what life throws at you).

We've got a whole lot of people out there who are watching us live out our faith in Jesus Christ during one of the biggest tests God has ever given us to pass. My prayer is that we don't fail Him. His Word has not changed from the one He gave me when our path seemed to be heading in a slightly different direction. That is, *"Be still, and know that I am God"* (Psalm 46:10). We are to *"fix our eyes on Jesus, the author and perfecter of our faith"* (Hebrews 12:2) as we make our way into the eye of this storm, where we will find Him waiting.

These updates are becoming nothing short of a "faith book" journal for me. Thank you all for allowing me to share my journey of faith with you.

Lisa (Mom)

Lifeline

"Consider it pure joy, my brothers, whenever you face trials of many kinds, because you know that the testing of your faith develops perseverance. Perseverance must finish its work so that you may be mature and complete, not lacking anything" (James 1:2–4).

"In this you greatly rejoice, though now for a little while you may have had to suffer grief in all kinds of trials. These have come so that your faith—of greater worth than gold, which perishes even though refined by fire—may be proved genuine and may result in praise, glory and honor when Jesus Christ is revealed" (1 Peter 1:6–7).

Prayer for Benjamin Elliott
Sunday, March 22, 2009

It's now been just over seven months since we began this journey, and over a week now since the news of Ben's relapse.

We are grieving the loss of Ben's physical health, along with all the obvious side effects of his disease: muscle loss, hair loss, puffy face from the steroids, head scar from the brain surgeries, mouth sores, aches and pains, among others. We are also experiencing the sorrow of our athlete son not being able to walk much farther than around the block without shortness of breath, let alone walking eighteen holes of golf.

We are grieving the loss of Ben's educational pursuits—for now. This is that wonderful time of year when students are receiving word of university and college acceptances. At the time of his diagnosis, Ben had been making plans to do a victory lap at his high school, leading his volleyball team to victory as captain of the team and taking some courses to enter into a nursing program in the fall.

We are grieving the loss of our family beach days. Because of the chemo, we'll have to be extra careful about sun exposure this summer. To add insult to injury, Ben will be unable to be immersed in the water due to the line that's inserted into his arm.

We are grieving the loss of our family vacation, as we have a figurative umbilical cord attached to the hospital, heading there two or three times a week on an indefinite basis.

We are grieving the loss of the life we once knew, knowing it will never be the same again.

We will never be the same again, but that's not a bad thing!

Because of all of this new life, we have a heightened sensitivity to those who have been or are on similar journeys and have been for years. We applaud them with a standing ovation.

Finding healing in the tears,
Lisa (Mom)

Lifeline

"The joy of the Lord is your strength" (Nehemiah 8:10).

Prayer for Benjamin Elliott
Tuesday, March 24, 2009

I will never forget one of the first good laughs we had after Ben's diagnosis back in August. He had been prone to all-day nose bleeds leading up to his diagnosis that were, unbeknownst to us at the time, one of the symptoms of his low platelets. Following his first transfusion, he had one of these nose bleeds. As he wiped his nose, he commented, "I thought I could taste somebody else's blood!"

The Ben Ripple

Well, it's true, right? With that first transfusion, he really *did* have somebody else's blood running through his veins—and probably right back out his nose! If you don't laugh, you cry!

Many, including nurses and doctors who have seen Ben at his worst, continue to comment on his positive attitude and dry sense of humor, which have truly kept us all going. There are very few times when we hear him complain.

Last night, as I was working upstairs in our home, I could hear my boys, Ben and Jacob, laughing, singing, and carrying on downstairs. I rarely get to witness these kinds of moments. I haven't heard them do this for quite some time. I didn't dare leave the room, because I was having too much fun listening to them and didn't want to interfere with the magic of the moment. The rest of the night turned into one of sporadic laughter and lightheartedness.

With all the medication that Ben has to ingest these days (eight to sixteen pills daily just to control his headache), it sure was therapeutic and did my heart good to have a taste of some good stuff!

I truly thank God for the healing we find in tears, but I'm also thanking Him for the gift of laughter. It sure is good medicine!

Lisa (Mom)

Lifeline

"A cheerful heart is good medicine" (Proverbs 17:22).

PRAYER JOURNAL ENTRY
Saturday, March 28, 2009

I found myself on the verge of tears all day yesterday. I didn't release any, which somewhat surprises me. We're facing so much unknown with Ben's cancer, and the effects of it never go away.

Last night, David and I talked about what a day away together or an overnight would look like and whether or not we'd find anything to talk about outside of Ben. We concluded that although we feel that with the right timing we could get away together, absolutely everything is tied to Ben right now. Anything we do is totally dependent on where he's at in his treatment, how he's feeling, and how we're doing in relation to all the above. There's virtually no planning ahead.

Prayer for Benjamin Elliott
Sunday, March 29, 2009

I recall that when we met with the bone marrow transplant team, Ben asked the doctor what the survival rate was for a bone marrow transplant. The doctor's very wise response spoke volumes to me: "Ben, you're either one hundred percent alive or you're dead. There's no such thing as being sixty percent alive."

I think that sometimes when things don't go quite as we plan, we go around living life only sixty percent alive, becoming victims rather than victors of our circumstances. I'm pretty sure that Jesus didn't give us life in order for us to live it anything short of one hundred percent to the fullest! John 10:10 says that He has come to give us abundant life!

I'm happy to say that Ben is not simply surviving this disease, but he is truly thriving!

These days, Ben is often escorted to what they call "the suite," where he can have privacy for painful procedures as well as some quiet recovery time afterwards. After one particular procedure, which took a little longer than any of us liked, with sweat on his brow the doctor said, "Thank you, Ben, for your patience."

Not missing a beat, Ben responded, "Well, Doctor, thank you for yours!"

This same oncologist shared with us that whenever he was asked how he was able to "doctor" Ben with all of his exceptions to the rules, his answer was prompt: "Ben makes it easy."

So well-known is Ben to the women behind the reception desk for his positive disposition that they made him a sign to put up in the room. It says, "Sweet Ben's Suite."

We thank God for all they've done to help us as a family, not only to survive, but to thrive.

Lisa (Mom)

Lifeline

> "The thief comes only to steal and kill and destroy; I have come that they may have life, and have it to the full" (John 10:10).

Prayer for Benjamin Elliott
Sunday, April 5, 2009

I just wanted to take time today to thank you all for praying us through this past week. Our two hurdle days were Friday, March 27 (which would have been the date of Ben's admission for his bone marrow transplant), and, of course, April 1 (which would have been his transplant date). We were able to get through the week unscathed, for the most part, and I was finally able to make myself go through the mountain of cleaning supplies, small household items, and non-perishable foods and snacks I had set aside to take to the apartment. My plan was to put them away for future reference.

Someone asked me recently what Ben's doing for fun these days. Food is still very fun for Ben. He's eating well enough (popcorn consistently being his main food of choice) and finds much inspiration from the Food Network, even taking initiative in the kitchen, kicking me out some days so he can provide the family with food extraordinaire à la Ben.

He spends a lot of time with his flight simulator, flying us all over the world (Disney, Africa, British Columbia—you name it, we've been there recently). He has taken some mini-excursions with his girlfriend, Sarah, and is looking forward to a couple of his friends being home from university this week so he can hang with them when he's up to it.

He's got his bike ready for takeoff once the weather settles enough and coincides with his energy level and headache pain. He's hoping that he can even hit some golf balls this season—once again, if he can muster the strength.

We're learning not to write anything in our day planners in pen. We're choosing not to focus on what *would* have been, knowing that God still resides in the moment. I personally don't want to miss out on anything He has in store for me by living life with my eyes focused on the rearview mirror.

Finding contentment with what is,

Lisa (Mom)

PRAYER JOURNAL ENTRY
Sunday, April 12, 2009
This gloriously sunny Easter weekend has caught me off guard with the darkness that has enveloped my soul.

On Good Friday, I was able to hold my emotions in check until after the morning service. David spoke on the fact that Jesus understands our pain and our sorrow. As Ben would say, "He just gets it, folks."

I'm heartbroken as I watch Ben suffer, having an idea of what some of the future holds. He's in a lot of discomfort. Dealing with a fissure and ingrown toenails and continually popping pills as directed. I got word Friday that he's to begin radiation in two weeks, which will treat his entire brain and central nervous system. It will be fifteen treatments. They'll max him out in order to hopefully kill his disease.

I've been given an opportunity to consider, on a level I've never had to before, the suffering that Jesus went through because of His love for me. I have entered into a realm of experience that I can only imagine Jesus' mother could have related to as she watched her own son suffer and ultimately be put to death on a cross. As much as she knew He was born to die, I don't think anything could have prepared her for that moment, which changed the course of history, any more than us for the phone call that changed our lives forever.

Lifeline

"I wait for the Lord, my soul waits, and in his word I put my hope"
(Psalm 130:5).

PRAYER JOURNAL ENTRY
Wednesday, April 22, 2009

Today I had a peek at what could be in our future. Greg, a twenty-one-year-old fellow patient who was diagnosed a month before Ben, is dying. He never did go into remission, although they found a match for him just after Ben's was found. During our visit with the doctor, he strongly encouraged me to go see Greg and his parents in the intensive care unit today. From the onset of our journey, I have wondered what the end could look like. Perhaps this was my opportunity to find out.

Ben asked how my visit went when we were on our way home from the hospital. I didn't go into any elaborate description of what I saw, but Ben's pretty discerning regardless and didn't ask any more questions when I told him I would be surprised if Greg made it through the weekend. It reminds me of how quickly the wind can change direction.

At the same time, it shows me just how much You're protecting my heart, how watching Ben in good health and high spirits masks the reality that lurks around the corner. I can't help but wonder, Lord, did You give me that glimpse to minister to Greg's family, or was it for my own benefit, to prepare my own heart for what lies ahead?

Lifeline

"I do not concern myself with great matters or things too wonderful for me. But I have stilled and quieted my soul" (Psalm 131:1–2).

. . .

It was Sunday afternoon, and we were hosting some visiting missionaries for lunch when the phone rang. It was Greg's mother, calling to tell me that Greg was gone. As I listened to her relay the news, I fought to keep my mind from going to a place of no return.

After our call ended, I returned to the lunch table in a blur of tears. I knew God would forgive me for hoping our company would leave sooner rather than later so I could grieve the loss of one who would surely be missed. It was a reality check, indeed!

. . .

Prayer for Benjamin Elliott
Friday, April 24, 2009
The reality of the past couple of weeks has left Ben feeling pretty lousy. It's been a rough week for many reasons.

First of all, Ben is sick and tired of being sick and tired. He's sick and tired of being unable to eat due to mouth sores and stomach issues. He's sick and tired due to not being able to sleep at night. He's sick and tired of not having the energy or motivation to get the exercise he knows he needs. He's sick and tired of taking his daily dosage of numerous pills.

But an even tougher pill to swallow is getting the news that one of our fellow cancer patients, Greg, passed away—a true reality check. All in all, Ben's spirits are low, and I can't blame him. It would seem that when Ben's down, we're all a little down.

It's a continual challenge to live in the moment, and I am reminded again of how important it is to *fix [my] eyes on Jesus, the author and perfecter of our faith, who for the joy set before him endured the cross*" (Hebrews 12:2).

As you think of us, please pray for daily endurance and strength.
Lisa (Mom)

Prayer for Benjamin Elliott
Friday, May 8, 2009

Thank you for the many who have been working the nightshift as far as praying for our family goes. We need God's strength even through the night, as our days don't seem to end, especially during the times when Ben's not doing so well. Right now is one of those times, and because of this we are requesting that he have no visitors. But we'll take all the prayer we can get, just to get us all through the night.

David and I are alternating night shifts, enabling one of us to be at Ben's side 24/7 and the other to be at home with the rest of the family. For the time being, the other kids seem to be okay with having only one of us around home. However, it's still an adjustment, especially for our youngest, who just wants our whole family to be together at home again.

Thankful to a God who works the night shift,

Lisa (Mom)

Lifeline

"I will lift up my eyes to the hills—where does my help come from? My help comes from the Lord, the Maker of heaven and earth. He will not let your foot slip—he who watches over you will not slumber; indeed, he who watches over Israel will neither slumber nor sleep. The Lord watches over you—the Lord is your shade at your right hand; the sun will not harm you by day, nor the moon by night. The Lord will keep you from all harm—he will watch over your life; the Lord will watch over your coming and going both now and forevermore" (Psalm 121:1–8).

Prayer for Benjamin Elliott
Saturday, May 16, 2009

The past weeks have taken a toll on all of us in various ways. Ben is home from the hospital again as of yesterday, and we thank you all for your prayers over this past long week and a half. The nurses keep kidding about putting me on the payroll. Had we remained at the hospital much longer, I was going to begin a small business of hospital tours!

We had our welcome home hair removal ceremony upon arrival, as Ben is getting tired of waking up to more hair on his pillow than remains on his head.

The Ben Ripple

This is now the second time that the radiation has forced Ben to showcase his bold and beautiful baldness.

The team felt that they had done all they could do in our hospital home for the time being. Ben is in pretty much the same condition as he was when he was admitted last Tuesday, minus another ten pounds—that's twenty in three weeks—but thankfully also minus the fever and nausea. He still contends with stomach cramping and his now seven-month-long headache, so he is again at "home, sick."

There are definite bonuses to being in our own home; however, there is always a hint of hospital homesickness upon return, especially on Ben's part. He is made to feel so at home at the hospital, with all the love and care and 24/7 attention literally at his fingertips with the push of a button. But once again we will make the necessary readjustments to make the house feel like home again. He who is flexible will not break!

Repeat after me, "There's no place like home!"

Lisa (Mom)

PRAYER JOURNAL ENTRY
Monday, May 18, 2009

I am so thankful that there is nowhere I can hide from You, Lord. Even to the ends of the earth, there You will find me (Psalm 139).

Yesterday at the hospital, I got on the elevator twice and forgot to press a floor number. Had I not been with David one of those times, I would have been suspended in midair for who knows how long before I clued in. In the other incident, fortunately someone on another floor needed the elevator, so it advanced upward, where I was left no choice but to openly confess my brainlessness. She laughed and said, "Don't you feel like you kind of zone out here?" I gave her an affirmative reply.

Similarly, I feel caught between two worlds right now. Our days are blurring together. I'm not sure how to continue to invest in everyone we meet at the hospital. Last night, I sobbed all the way home and into the evening, awaking much the same way. Now, after a good walk around the river and enjoying the sunshine of my own backyard, I feel a little less emotional. I'm coming to a place where I need to grieve the loss of the many people at the hospital who will not necessarily be a part of my life once this part of our journey is over.

My mind has taken me to life without Ben over the past twenty-four hours, even though there is nothing in his appearance that indicates he's anywhere close to leaving us. Father, thank You that You know my needs even better than I know them. Thank You that You meet me where I'm at. Draw me close to You, Heavenly Father.

Lifeline

> "Come near to God and he will come near to you" (James 4:8). "The Spirit helps us in our weakness. We do not know what we ought to pray for, but the Spirit himself intercedes for us with groans that words cannot express" (Romans 8:26).

• • •

All was going well, with one clear finding to go. In fact, Ben was feeling better than he had in months. David had a week of holidays, so he joined Ben and me as we headed to the clinic for Ben's routine blood work. We decided to make it more of an "outing," which included purchasing a new unfinished dresser for the boys' room. Ben wanted a project for the three men of the house to work on together.

I remember taking inventory of Ben's blood counts that day and noted that they were much higher than usual, to the degree that I wondered if they'd gotten his results mixed up with someone else's. I let the dark cloud pass and left the clinic to go purchase a dresser. Ben picked out one that was suitable, and we told the salesperson we'd be back in two days to retrieve it. The mood was high as we left the store, so we picked up a pizza and took it to the airport to watch the planes land and take off, one of Ben's favorite things to do.

I opted to stay home from the clinic two days later in order to make room for the dresser. Partway through the afternoon, David called with news that once again rocked my world. Ben had experienced another relapse. We were already living out Plan B! What was *this* all about? Could there be a Plan C?

• • •

Prayer for Benjamin Elliott
Wednesday, May 27, 2009
As I write you today, I sit in a haze of disbelief, for lack of a better term. I just received yet another phone call, this time from my husband, who escorted Ben down to the cancer clinic today for his regular treatment. His counts had

recovered significantly over the weekend, allowing us to simply enjoy life for a few days.

However, the wind has changed direction again, and today blood tests have come back showing Ben has had what is called a "systemic relapse." In a nutshell, this means that the leukemia has returned to his blood and bone marrow, which means that we are back to the very beginning—only worse, in that not only do we know more than we did when Ben was first diagnosed, but we are once again reminded of just how aggressive this chromosome shift is.

Ben will be readmitted to the hospital as soon as they can make a bed available for him. He will begin a new regimen of chemotherapy as early as tomorrow. It is called the "salvage" treatment. Doesn't sound too pretty, does it? This inpatient treatment will carry on for the next month, or until remission can once again be attained. If remission can be attained, then the transplant hospital will be notified immediately, and plans will be made to get Ben in for a bone marrow transplant ASAP rather than waiting the six months that was in the original plan.

I am continuing to hold fast to Jesus Christ, the Anchor during this relentless storm in our lives.

Lisa (Mom)

Lifeline

"God is our refuge and strength, an ever-present help in trouble. Therefore we will not fear, though the earth give way and the mountains fall into the heart of the sea... 'Be still, and know that I am God; I will be exalted among the nations, I will be exalted in the earth.' The Lord Almighty is with us; the God of Jacob is our fortress" (Psalm 46:1–2, 10–11).

PRAYER JOURNAL ENTRY
Thursday, May 28, 2009

Well, Lord, here we are again. Not just You and I together again, but here in the hospital. Ben had a systemic relapse yesterday. I'm still a little numb. It's a different feeling this time around. Originally back in August, it was surreal. When he had his relapse in March, it was a "You're kidding me, right?" This time it's just a lump in the gut that kinda lodges itself where either it could make me vomit or it rides between my heart and my throat. There is a heaviness in my chest that can only slightly be alleviated or relieved with heaving sobs.

Prayer for Benjamin Elliott
Sunday, May 31, 2009
David and Ben were reminded again on Wednesday by our oncologist, in a number of ways, that all odds continue to work against Ben. We have been made aware of this from the very beginning when it was discovered that he was at high risk due to this chromosome shift we continue to mention.

We were told right from the start that it was highly unlikely that he would go into remission and, if he were to, the chances of him relapsing were equally as high. Now that Ben has had another relapse, odds are that much more against him. It will be an absolute miracle if Ben can go into remission again, but that is exactly what we're praying for.

We *know* and believe without a shadow of a doubt that God is absolutely *able* to do above and beyond what we can even begin to think or imagine (Ephesians 3:20). However, we don't have the mind of the Lord to know if He is *willing* to heal Ben. We have been living with this reality right from the start, and we have to be okay with whatever the Lord decides.

Thank you for joining us in prayer for an utter miracle against all odds.
Lisa (Mom)

Lifeline

> "He makes my feet like the feet of a deer; he enables me to stand on the heights. He trains my hands for battle… You give me your shield of victory, and your right hand sustains me" (Psalm 18:33–35).

Keeping Your Marriage Alive When Your Child is Dying

Statistics show that ninety percent of all couples experiencing the terminal illness or death of a child have serious marital problems. Sixty percent divorce or separate within two years. Three out of four divorce within six years.

Having an idea of some of the adverse effects that a family crisis has on a marriage helped to build our resolve to keep our marriage intact and fight for its survival. Here are some of the things we found helpful in keeping our marriage strong.

- Make intentional time together.
- Take time to talk about the situation, your other children, and how you're coping personally.
- Be sensitive to each other's varying needs.
- Date. Every night, David and I had a mini-date for ten minutes when he walked me from the hospital back to the hotel. We used this time to debrief and touch base personally.
- Let go of the little things… because the little things will get to you!
- Accept that you both have strengths to offer, rather than being intimidated or feeling that both of you have to be good at *everything*.
- Don't rely solely on your mate to make you feel better again.
- Discuss your feelings and opinions openly with each other.
- Give each other space to deal with the situation in your personal way.
- Expect agitation and blowups.
- Don't neglect intimacy.
- Be okay with your spouse's odd malfunction day. Menial tasks can be debilitating, overwhelming, and unconquerable. Stress, loss, and grief can be paralyzing. Emotions run high when a couple is under stress. Therefore be understanding towards each other when those times occur.
- Make your marriage your top priority. It's a gift to your children.
- Make time for each other, no matter how you're feeling emotionally.

PRACTICAL TIPS (con't.)

- Find an "away place" for just the two of you where you're free to have privacy.
- Don't criticize your spouse's coping mechanisms (unless they are unhealthy).
- Seek professional help if necessary.

Ben (age 3) leading house guests in singing, "Holy, Holy, Holy.
Lord God *on my team*."

Seizing a moment during the Elliotts' big family trip to Disney World, Florida.
(March, 2006) (Left to right – Jacob, Ben, Erin, David, Natalie, Lisa)

Ben giving a pep talk to the boys' senior volleyball team. (Jacob is #4)

Ben and Lisa cooking up a Thai dinner. (Spring 2008)

Ben's prom. (June, 2008 – six weeks before his diagnosis)

"The Perfect Match" Ben and Sarah - Ben's Prom, (June, 2008)

Ben appeasing a steroid-induced craving following his first brain surgery to insert the "Ommaya". (October, 2008)

BenFest; an organized fundraiser for the Elliott's. (October, 2008)
(Left to right – Natalie, Jacob, David, Erin, Ben, Lisa)

A "Kodak moment of the heart" at Ben's high school commencement.
(November, 2008)

Ben's visit with the Kindergarten class who prayed faithfully for Ben's "bows and
arrows transplant." (December, 2008)

Ben boarding a plane to visit family. (March, 2009)

Ben (holding his radiation mask) and Abby, the radiation technician.
(October, 2008)

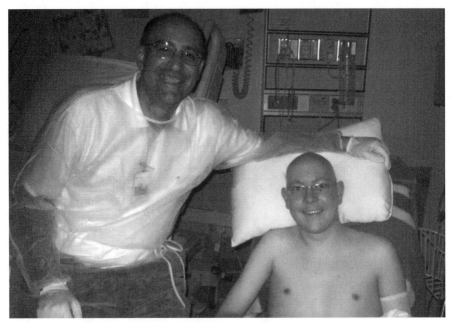

Ben and "Dr. Axe." (July, 2009)

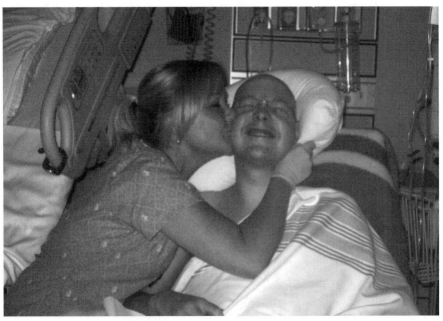

Nurse Megan lovin` on Ben. (July, 2009)

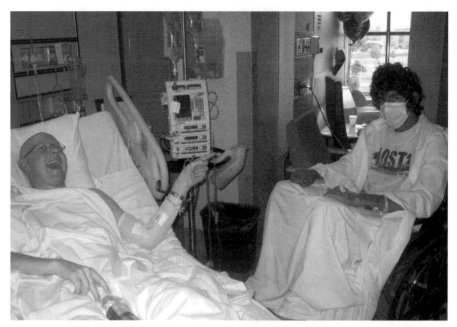

"A series of unfortunate events." Ben and Jacob's reunion after Jacob was admitted into hospital. (July, 2009)

Ben's fulfillment of a dream; flying a plane. (July, 2009)

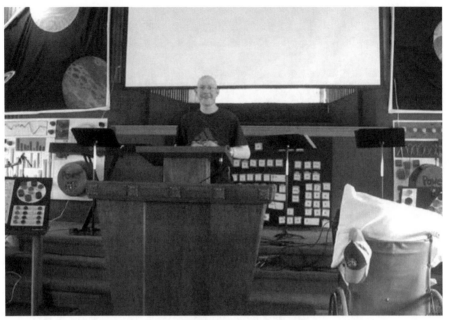

Ten days before he died, Ben delivered what many said to be the "best sermon" they'd ever heard. (August 9, 2009)

Ben, Sarah and Erin feeding the ducks two days before he died. (August, 2009)

Seeing Natalie off at the airport two days after Ben's funeral.
(Left to right – Lisa, Jacob, David, Erin, Natalie)

The "Ben Bell" (donated to the cancer clinic fall 2009) was the fulfillment of Ben's wish for patients to have a "real" bell to ring to celebrate the completion of their chemo treatments.

Lisa and Susan (Ben's nurse practitioner) sharing a coffee together on Ben's memorial bench (November, 2011).

The plaque on the memorial bench placed in October, 2011 in Ben's memory outside of Family & Co. toy store in Stratford, Ontario.

CHAPTER 8

When THE WHEELS COME OFF

The countenance of Ben's oncologist, as well as that of Susan, his nurse practitioner, was heavy as they took seats at Ben's bedside. The air hung thick as we awaited the news of whether or not the most recent treatment had been successful. Then, when the doctor gave us the unbearable news, it was as if a vacuum sucked the remaining air from the room. Not only was the treatment unsuccessful in bringing Ben into remission, but with this news came our biggest reality check yet: *Ben had days, maybe weeks, to live.*

Dr. "Axe", as always, was straight with us. He looked at Ben and played out the scenario of what his final days could be like. He said, "Ben, when the wheels start to come off, my suggestion is that we don't resuscitate you." He went on to say that this simply prolonged the process and it was never pleasant. When Ben agreed, the doctor said, "We've just taken care of a matter that often takes hours to resolve at the most inopportune time. Good call, Ben."

When the wheels start to come off? What did that look like? Was this discussion even taking place? After a little more information about Ben's options, we were left alone to process the news. Ben had days, maybe weeks, to live? I would need at least that much time to process this devastating blow.

• • •

The Ben Ripple

Prayer for Benjamin Elliott
Thursday, June 18, 2009

Yesterday we got news that there would be no need for a bone marrow biopsy to check for any leukemia in Ben's blood. The most recent blood work had shown them everything they needed to know; there were leukemia blasts throughout Ben's blood, meaning that the treatment he just underwent didn't work and didn't achieve the remission we were hoping for. Our oncologist wanted to meet with us later in the day to discuss "our options."

Our options, we learned, were limited.

Option #1: Supportive care, which consists of ongoing transfusions and antibiotics to keep Ben from suffering. Due to the aggression of the leukemia, this option could keep him alive for potentially days, maybe only weeks.

Option #2: A new chemotherapy treatment from the States that even our team isn't fully familiar with. There is less than 10 percent chance of success, but if it works, it could extend Ben's life.

Once the doctor had explained these options and we had the opportunity to ask some questions, Ben did something that he hasn't done since last summer after he collapsed at work and then couldn't climb up the three steps leading into our home; he cried.

Both Natalie and Erin came to the hospital shortly thereafter, and each shed their tears alongside David and me before we made the decision to bring Ben home for the night, where we could be together as a family and consider our options. Ben could also tell his brother, Jacob, and Sarah the news in person.

Jacob's initial response was God's divine way of speaking truth to each of our hearts. "Well, Ben, in a twisted kind of way, we can all actually be a little envious…" In other words: "Ben, you may get to see Jesus before the rest of us." Then he proceeded to pick up his guitar and play some worship songs, ministering to us all while we sat around as a family singing, weeping, and laughing together.

One of Jacob's song selections was "Praise You in This Storm," by Casting Crowns. Given the fact that it had been raining all day and on our way home from the hospital, I believe the raindrops were some of God's own tears being shed on our behalf. Partway home, the sun began to peek out enough that a full rainbow spread itself across the entire sky. At one point, the end of it landed squarely on the road ahead. As we watched it in wonder, we all agreed that this was God's assurance to us of the hope we can continue to have in Him—in Christ alone.

Please be praying for wisdom for all of us. Although it is ultimately up to Ben which option he chooses, we of course will be guiding him through the decision with much prayer, seeking wisdom from on high. For now, we are heading back to the hospital. No matter which option he chooses, Ben needs to be assured that we will stand with him.

Lisa (Mom)

Lifeline

> "He tends his flock like a shepherd: He gathers the lambs in his arms and carries them close to his heart; he gently leads those that have young" (Isaiah 40:11).

Prayer for Benjamin Elliott
Friday, June 19, 2009

I apologize for having left you all hanging over the past twenty-four hours. After a very intense and heavy time of deliberation, we arrived back at the hospital midafternoon yesterday still not having made a decision. It was very evident that it was weighing heavily on Ben, so it was a relief when our doctor made an appearance shortly after our arrival to present his own thoughts, after a very intense deliberation of his own through the night.

He laid things out very clearly once again but this time with a new resolve as he informed Ben that he felt that he was willing to make a go of the chemo route if Ben was agreeable. Both he and Ben concluded that he will at least have a chance of heading into remission with the chemo route, whereas the other option gives him no hope whatsoever. We were again assured that he will be given the best care possible and will not be left to suffer either way.

Trusting Jesus with every step we take,

Lisa (Mom)

Prayer Journal Entry
Sunday, June 21, 2009

Psalm 27:13–14 says, *"I am still confident of this: I will see the goodness of the Lord in the land of the living. Wait for the Lord; be strong and take heart and wait for the Lord."*

This is the cry of my heart today, Lord: sure confidence in You. I would love to think that You will heal Ben and put him into remission here on earth, but I have to keep in mind that we on earth are in the land of the dying, while heaven is the land where living *really* takes place. Either way, Lord, I will wait for You. I will be strong and take heart, and I will wait for You.

I woke up with this resolve. No tears, just a strength I knew I needed, not only for myself but for Ben. David woke up much the same. Lord, lead us victoriously over these next days.

Prayer for Benjamin Elliott
Wednesday, June 24, 2009

As I write to you today, Ben's fourth day of chemo is in progress, and he is sleeping right through it. Yeah!

At the start of this journey, God gave both David and me a key word. For David, it was the word "mercy," and for me it was the word "glory." When David has been praying for God to be merciful, he's really been asking for God to display His mercy by healing Ben of cancer. God may still do that, but we both also realize that His mercy may be demonstrated by choosing to stop Ben's suffering and taking him to his ultimate home. Both ways, God is merciful, and we will trust Him.

All along, I have sensed that this situation with Ben is much bigger than Ben and our family. Somehow this has all been about God's glory. Already God has been incredibly glorified, as many have been impacted by Ben's story around the world. If Ben ultimately dies, only eternity will reveal the countless lives that have been touched and changed because of his journey. We believe there will be people in heaven because of his suffering.

To the ends of the earth!

Lisa (Mom)

• • •

Ben confided in me and his dad that of all the days of his illness, the day he felt the most sick was his nineteenth birthday. He was in head-to-toe pain and asked for his pain medication more frequently.

As his dad sat at his side and I massaged his aching legs and feet, relief slowly began to set in, allowing him to drift off to sleep.

Our church family ordered and sent a birthday cake large enough to serve all the hospital staff on our floor and then some. However, it wasn't until later that day that we were finally able to get Ben out of bed. We rallied all our friends, family, nurses, and staff in a gathering place on the floor and sang to him, allowing him to make the first cut in the cake. Then, at his request, we quickly wheeled him back to his room. It was obvious to David and me that making an appearance had little to do with himself and everything to do with showing his appreciation to those who had gathered.

Later that night, as his dad lay on the pullout chair beside his bed, Ben said, "Dad, I don't want to disappoint you when I say this, but today when the medication kicked in and you and Mom were both with me…" He paused. "I just wanted to close my eyes and…" Another pause.

David finished the thought for him and said, "You wanted to fall asleep here and wake up there" (Referring to heaven).

Ben gave an affirmative, then said again, "I hope you're not disappointed."

Although he had kept his attitude in check all through the months of his illness, Ben was now coming to terms with "the end." He was accepting his possible fate and letting us in on it.

Disappointed? How could we be anything but proud of him?

· · ·

Lifeline

"As the deer pants for streams of water, so my soul pants for you, O God… Why are you downcast, O my soul? Why so disturbed within me? Put your hope in God, for I will yet praise him, my Savior and my God" (Psalm 42:1, 5–6).

Prayer for Benjamin Elliott
Tuesday, July 7, 2009

It occurred to David and me last night as we were having our daily debriefing time just how life has changed over the past eleven months, how the "new normal" has evolved into "normal normal." What once was considered a bad day is now actually a good day. We commented on the fact that it is nice to see Ben having a good day after a chain of not-so-good ones. Then, when we stopped to think about what constituted his "good day," we did a double take. His good day yesterday consisted of getting over his nausea. By the time evening came around, with the help of his increased pain medication, he was able to sit up in a wheelchair long enough for us to go outside (for the first time in over eight days) to feed some birds in one of the hospital's healing gardens.

The Ben Ripple

It is getting increasingly difficult to watch our precious Benjamin suffer. I find strength and consolation in the fact that our Heavenly Father totally understands and feels our pain, as He, too, watched His own Son suffer. Although He never promised that life would be easy, He *has* promised His presence throughout our journey… and *that* is worth hanging on to!

This is the day that the Lord has made. We *will* rejoice and be glad in it!

Lisa (Mom)

Lifeline

"When I said, 'My foot is slipping,' your love, O Lord, supported me. When anxiety was great within me, your consolation brought joy to my soul... But the Lord has become my fortress, and my God the rock in whom I take refuge" (Psalm 94:18–19, 22).

. . .

Golf was a favorite pastime for Ben, his brother, and their dad. One very early morning in the hospital when neither David nor Ben could sleep, David looked outside to see the sun rising. He said, "Ben, this would be a *great* day to play a round of golf." So they did! Of course, it wasn't on an actual golf course, but rather right there in their beds. They even kept track of their score, tying their game with a virtual 77!

Ben always looked forward to daily hospital rounds, although not quite as much as a round of golf. It was a chance for him to ask any questions that might be brewing in his ever-curious and alert mind. He loved to kibitz with the members of his team, and it also gave him a reason to harass me for my rambling ways. If nothing else, it made for a lot of interesting conversation.

On July 20, 2009, the team had already been by to see Ben, but this day they came for one *final* round…

. . .

Prayer for Benjamin Elliott
Monday, July 20, 2009
Today is day thirty of Ben's most recent treatment, and his counts this morning were finally high enough to perform a bone marrow aspirate.

We weren't expecting to hear results until tomorrow, identifying whether or not Ben is in remission. However, our team returned a little while ago to give us news that this last round of chemotherapy was not effective in bringing Ben back into remission. Ninety percent of his cells were leukemic blasts.

We'll know in the next few days how aggressively the cancer is progressing. Alongside our hematology oncology team, we'll come up with a plan as to how to keep him comfortable for the rest of the days God has ordained for him.

I can't put my feelings down any better than what has already been said by the late Ruth Bell Graham: "I lay my 'whys?' before Your cross in worship kneeling, my mind beyond all hope, my heart beyond all feeling; and worshipping, realize that I in knowing You, don't need a 'why?'."[1]

To the glory of God,
Lisa (Mom)

Lifeline

"Even in darkness light dawns for the upright... He will have no fear of bad news; his heart is steadfast, trusting in the Lord. His heart is secure, he will have no fear" (Psalm 112:4, 7–8).

Prayer for Benjamin Elliott
Tuesday, July 21, 2009

What does the morning after the day before look like? There have been many tears, and likely there will be many more to come. There have been many questions, but there has also been a true sense of the peace and presence of God in our midst.

I also feel impressed to share with you, on this morning after, that Ben is not afraid of dying. He is not afraid, because he has a personal relationship with the Lord Jesus Christ. As a result, he has a hope that transcends the grave—hope that after his leaving this earth, he will enter into the glorious presence of his Savior.

I would be remiss to not say that the thought of the dying process isn't a little scary for all of us. We have many questions as to what it will look like and how we should handle the last leg of this journey. We ask you to pray that Ben's last days/weeks will be well-spent, that as we take the necessary time to consider things that Ben still wants to accomplish before God takes him home, that God

[1] Anne Graham Lotz, *Why?* (Nashville, TN: Thomas Nelson, 2004), p. xvii.

will grant him the desires of his heart, and that we will share much laughter along with our tears.

Pray that we will make new and lasting memories as we continue our journey on this earth together.

Lisa (Mom)

Lifeline

"Therefore we do not lose heart. Though outwardly we are wasting away, yet inwardly we are being renewed day by day. For our light and momentary troubles are achieving for us an eternal glory that far outweighs them all. So we fix our eyes not on what is seen, but on what is unseen. For what is seen is temporary, but what is unseen is eternal" (2 Corinthians 4:16–18).

. . .

We kept a very open line of communication with Ben. Some people were shocked at our "open heart/open mouth policy," but what they didn't know was that Ben led the charge. Whenever he initiated conversation and wanted to explore the depths of his condition or meager prognosis, we followed suit. While we engaged in the reality of death, we were always careful to speak words of life to him.

. . .

PRAYER JOURNAL ENTRY
Friday, July 24, 2009
The other day, Ben and I shared some alone time together. It was the first time in over a month. Even when it's only David and me with Ben, we're often both here together with him.

I can't remember how, but we began talking about what heaven will be like. He wanted to know my opinion on it and whether I felt all we'd do is gaze at Jesus, similar to the words of the song "I Can Only Imagine" by his favorite group, Mercy Me.

I told him I believe that once we see Jesus' face, it will likely satisfy us for the rest of eternity, but we may want to stop and stare for a while. Then, although we've all got mansions waiting for us, he asked if I thought Jesus would let us be on our own every now and then so we could visit with each other from mansion to mansion. We both laughed at this.

He told me that sometimes in his sleep lately, he's seen the colors of heaven and how indescribable they are. Apparently they're nothing like colors here on earth. Somehow, we then got talking about when he and the other kids were little, how we would carefully choose a babysitter whenever his dad and I went out on dates. As long as I knew the kids were in good hands and I could trust the babysitter, I could go and enjoy myself.

Then I drew the comparison of entrusting him to Jesus, knowing that although it will be hard, I can go on enjoying life trusting that I am leaving him in good hands. Ben said that he and his dad had had a similar conversation lately, and his dad had told him that our children are on loan to us from God. Then Ben went on to say, "So, in fact, Mom, you are the babysitter!"

Yes, indeed. Lord, You have entrusted me with my children until You want to reclaim them for Yourself. I will sadly, but gladly, give Ben back to You, Father. I certainly trust You, but maybe I should be saying thank You for trusting me!

Lisa (Mom)

How to Prepare Your Loved One for Death

Death is a difficult subject to talk about. Therefore it is easy to *avoid* talking about it. However, I believe that by doing so we miss out on some of the most intimate conversations we could ever have.

We were fortunate that Ben often broached the subject at his own initiative. The fact is, we all have questions and concerns brewing deep inside us. So, for those who are looking for ways to enter into discussion with those coming to the end of their earthly existence, here are some ways to approach it.

- Don't be afraid to address the tough issues.
- Encourage him or her to live purposefully. Ben attempted a computer course and piano lessons, flew a plane, shared his heart with our church family, and savored moments with his girlfriend and other friends.
- Ask him or her about hopes, fears, and feelings.
- Continue to dream with him or her (without giving false hope).
- Hope for the best while being prepared for the worst. This helps everyone involved to keep a healthy balance between optimism and pessimism.
- Celebrate small victories.
- Be honest about what is going on. Silence leaves room for speculation, wrong assumptions, and unnecessary fears.
- Answer his or her questions as fully as he or she is able to comprehend or grasp.
- Take his or her lead in conversation. If he or she wants to talk about things like death, funerals, or matters that might seem morbid to you… let him or her. He or she obviously feels the need to explore such things.
- Don't be afraid to show your emotions. It will permit him or her to feel and express his or her own.
- Keep him or her company. It gives an extra dose of assurance that he or she isn't alone (physically or emotionally).

PRACTICAL TIPS (con't.)

- Give him or her the space he or she needs (while keeping him or her informed of your whereabouts and availability).
- Ask him or her what he or she needs/wants/expects of you.
- Come up with a "code" for unwanted or overextended visitors, to help alleviate stress.
- Talk about heaven.
- Celebrate special occasions.
- Don't prevent him or her from expressing his or her raw feelings and frustrations.
- Keep your other children in the loop.
- Be present.
- Live in the moment!

CHAPTER 9

Pushed TO THE LIMIT

Knowing the uncertainty we faced, it was with much apprehension that we allowed our son Jacob to go four hours away to work at a camp for the summer. (This is the same camp he had been at when he received word of Ben's diagnosis the summer before.) He had also been planning a weekend camping trip with a friend. It unfortunately happened to be the weekend that we received word of Ben's grim prognosis.

It was imperative that we get Jacob to see his brother ASAP, so the juggling began... again. It wasn't until the van was loaded and they were heading down the highway that Jacob began complaining of a red, itchy rash. Before too long, he started to experience a fever and involuntary twitching. David decided to pull off the highway and go to the nearest hospital emergency. He was sent on his way after being told to take some Tylenol and use some Benadryl for the itch.

The next day, back at home, Jacob's symptoms worsened, so David brought him to our local hospital emergency. They were considering admitting him until David informed them of what was going on with Ben an hour away—so they instead decided to keep him on observation long enough to see if the steroids would take effect. He was discharged within a few hours.

In the meantime, I happened to mention this new development to a fellow Facebook sojourner who was a doctor at the emergency department at the hospital where Ben was. She advised us to get a third opinion from the "Rash Queen," a specialist in the field of skin rashes. All I knew was that we needed to gather our family together in one place as quickly as possible! Our time as a whole family was running out.

Overnight, Jacob's rash began developing into blisters all over his body. Upon examination, the Rash Queen told David that as ill as Ben was, if Jacob wasn't treated immediately he could be in worse shape than Ben. Now we had two boys on death row. Did God not know there was a limit to what we could endure? No script could ever compete with our new reality.

• • •

Lifeline

"Those who trust in the Lord are like Mount Zion, which cannot be shaken but endures forever" (Psalm 125:1).

Prayer for Benjamin Elliott
Friday, July 24, 2009

This morning, Jacob's now head-to-toe rash began to blister, so David headed down to the emergency department for a third day, this time at Ben's hospital. Jacob was introduced to the Rash Queen before being admitted. We should know in a couple of days what exactly we're dealing with. The worst part of this saga is that this means Jacob is not able to come to see his brother until we figure things out.

It just so happens that Jacob is situated on the same floor as Ben, just around the corner in the pediatric ward! Just to let you know how ludicrous this entire scenario is, across the entire border surrounding the ceiling are the words "Once Upon A Time… Happily Ever After." Hmmm. Maybe the reality is more like the way Ben defines it: "A Series of Unfortunate Events"!

If nothing else, we're still finding laughter to be the best medicine.
Lisa (Mom)

Prayer for Benjamin Elliott
Sunday, July 26, 2009

Lying awake these past couple of nights since Jacob's admission, gazing at the fluffy clouds painted on the ceiling, butterflies, blue skies, and a mural of a castle on the walls, I can't help but wonder if I'm living out a fairy tale or a nightmare.

I'm caught in this surreal world where I don't know some moments whether I should be laughing hysterically, sobbing uncontrollably, or vomiting.

While time ticks away for Ben, who is now receiving blood products daily, Jacob's rash continues to grow. What began as a small itchy rash on his arms has developed into huge blisters that now cover his entire body, including inside his mouth.

The staff at the hospital, both in Ben's cancer ward and Jacob's pediatric ward, have agreed that the boys are permitted to visit one another as they each feel up to it. So the boys have now had two visits—each taking their turn to host. We have taken advantage of the opportunity to capture the encounters on camera and video. Otherwise, no one would believe what is being lived out before our eyes.

Just picture bald Ben lying in a bed attached to an IV pole with numerous bags suspended from it, and sitting next to him is hairy Jacob in a wheelchair, wrapped in swaddling clothes and plugged into an IV pole all his own. The bantering between the two of them as they compared notes and shared war wounds was actually music to our ears, bringing much laughter mixed with sadness.

Please continue to pray Ben remains comfortable and doesn't suffer as he prepares to meet Jesus. Pray that Jacob will also be kept comfortable and stable so that we can have more family gatherings.

A little rattled, but not totally shaken,

Lisa (Mom)

Prayer Journal Entry
Thursday, July 30, 2009

What a pity party I had all day yesterday! Tears, pouting, confusion, conflict! Sleep deprivation isn't helping my cause right now. I'm vulnerable, sensitive, irritable, and exhausted! I crawled into bed last night with the lingering effects of the day. I'm so thankful, Lord, that You met me there, wiped my tears, took my face in Your hands, and asked me why on earth, after all You've done in my midst, I would suddenly feel the right to look inward instead of upward!

Thank You, Lord, for reminding me that it's *not about me!*

The Ben Ripple

Prayer for Benjamin Elliott
Thursday, July 30, 2009
Here's a good recipe for prayer:

MAIN INGREDIENTS: 1 Elliott Family (equal to 6 uniquely created children of God).

BLEND IN: 1 loyal girlfriend (Ben's secret ingredient).

GINGERLY COMBINE: everyone's individual needs.

MIX TOGETHER: 4 separate living quarters, sleep deprivation, emotional exhaustion, 1 large quantity of heartache.

GENTLY FOLD IN: coordination and orchestration of room-to-room visits based upon timing of IV meds, energy to make the trip down the hall, wheelchair searches, and mask and glove supply due to health precautions.

ADD SPORADICALLY: daily visits from a large variety of medical professionals such as hematology oncologists, infectious disease specialists, dermatologists, ophthalmologists, wound specialists, and pharmacists.

GENEROUSLY APPLY: prayer warriors (Colossians 4:2–4), the joy of the Lord, which is our strength (Nehemiah 8:10), wisdom from God's Word (2 Timothy 3:16–17), and trust in God who is able to do exceedingly abundantly beyond what we can ask or imagine (Ephesians 3:20).

LET SIMMER DAILY IN GOD'S PRESENCE (Acts 2:28).

YIELDS: contentment in our circumstances (Philippians 4:11), peace beyond our comprehension (Philippians 4:7), and abundant fruit in its season (Jeremiah 17:7–8).

Enjoy and savor the flavor,
Lisa (Mom)

. . .

Jacob's in-hospital stay ended up being ten days. His diagnosis was never conclusive, so we just chalked it up as a means by which God turned our series of unfortunate events into some irreplaceable and memorable moments together.

CHAPTER 10

Dancing
IN THE RAIN

How do you address life issues when life is cut short? How do you talk about the reality of the end when the end has not yet come? How do you face the reality of tomorrow when you still have to live today?

Living like we were dying, as the song goes, wasn't so much about skydiving or Rocky Mountain climbing as much as it was about making each and every moment we had together count. Laughing when we felt like it, crying when we needed to, and dreaming together even knowing that the dreams might never come to pass. Isn't that what dreaming is about, after all? We chose to get the most out of life while we still had life to live together.

Just like Ben and I had discussed that beautiful fall day on our way to the clinic, Ben chose to live purposefully. He wanted to live life to the fullest, in whatever way that took shape. David and Ben came up with a list that David wrote on Ben's hospital whiteboard of "things to do," "things to say," and "people to see" before he breathed his last breath. Even if God stepped in at the very last minute to save Ben, which we knew He could, why not do and say anything and everything we could so that either way there was no room for regrets?

We came across an anonymous quote that said, "Life is not about waiting for the storm to pass; it's learning to dance in the rain." It was an appropriate quote for us, as the weather turned out to be the rainiest year on record. In a very real sense, we faced the biggest storm in our lives.

The Ben Ripple

It was evident as Ben's suffering increased that so, too, did God's grace, enabling Ben to have some extraordinary experiences. Even in the final days of his life, Ben's determination and will to live to the fullest won out. Our family followed Ben's lead as he taught us all what it meant to truly "dance in the rain."

. . .

Lifeline

"'My grace is sufficient for you, for my power is made perfect in weakness.' Therefore I will boast all the more gladly about my weaknesses, so that Christ's power may rest on me. That is why, for Christ's sake, I delight in weaknesses, in insults, in hardships, in persecutions, in difficulties. For when I am weak, then I am strong" (2 Corinthians 12:9–10).

Prayer for Benjamin Elliott
Friday, July 31, 2009
The other day, our church family and community gathered in our church parking lot to watch as Ben flew a plane over them. Unfortunately, the flight had to be cancelled due to weather. However, I'm pleased to say that yesterday, both the weather and Ben's health aligned in such a way that Ben was able to fulfill one of his all-time goals: to fly a plane. That's right! After a very sleepless night and a very nauseous morning, yet again Ben's determination won out, and he was able to take his girlfriend and youngest sister on a four-seat aircraft for an hour. And, yes, you heard right… after years of flight simulating, Ben was able to actually *fly* the plane with the pilot as his co-pilot! So cool! David and I left Natalie at the hospital with Jacob and were able to watch the plane taxi and then take off with joy flooding our souls and tears flooding our eyes. Such a gift!
Lisa (Mom)

Prayer Journal Entry
Saturday, August 1, 2009
Last night, Ben had another fever. His headache is nonstop. His nausea comes and goes. He's started to experience ringing in his ears, and he's got weird hiccup things going on. He now has a pump for pain control.
He has been planning his funeral and putting thoughts on paper, download-

116

ing songs onto a CD to be played. Today he wants to go home to see a few friends and "get his things in order." Lord, my heart breaks to think we're here. We're really living this!

Some of the words that come to mind when I think of Ben are: strong-willed but sensitive, protective (especially of his siblings), discerning, thoughtful, honest, generous, smart, self-motivated, meditative, pensive, calculating, conversational, athletic, full of integrity, committed, theologically sound, a born leader, determined, relentless, persistent, observant, gracious, pleasant, polite, stubborn, mischievous, and unaffectionate but very lovable. He possesses a dry sense of humor and is always thinking ahead.

I love him so very much!

Prayer for Benjamin Elliott
Wednesday, August 5, 2009
Along with Ben's flight, another great escape we had this week was that of both boys being able to get a leave of absence, enabling us to enjoy a barbecue in a nearby park. The sight of the two brothers wearing ball caps, hospital face masks, and gloves while shuffling side by side cloaked in white sheets gave us not only a good laugh, but also the privacy we needed. There was no way anyone wanted to get close enough to catch whatever it was people guessed we had!

Yet another great escape was all of us being able to go home for a night as a family. Ben was given the blood products he needed early in the day and sent home with all the necessary drugs to get him through the night. What a wonderful thing to experience… all of us in one place, in our own beds, eating our own food, enjoying each other's company… in our own home!

Lisa (Mom)

• • •

Ben truly *lived* in every moment, including just ten days before he died when he did something that was nothing short of a miracle! In fact, I would call it Ben's *finest* moment. He was given a leave of absence from the hospital for the night because he had some things on his heart that he wanted to share with our church family the next morning.

So, after waking him up in time so he could rise slowly and look over the notes he had carefully prepared, we made our way to the church. No one was expecting to see us, let alone that Ben would stand behind the pulpit and give a message that will not soon be forgotten! I like to call it the "*Ben*ediction."

The Benediction:

BEN'S FINAL WORDS TO OUR CHURCH FAMILY

Good morning!

It's good to be here and to see everyone again. It's been quite a long time, and to be honest I didn't know if the day would come again, but it's good to be back—finally!

I'm not going to be very long this morning because I'm kind of weak, I have a pounding headache, and I'm a little nauseous, to be honest with you.

I don't want to have this morning focus on me at all. In fact, I was quite hesitant to even do this because I thought that by me coming up here it would be focusing this whole past year on me, and that's the exact opposite of what I want. This whole past year has been about God entirely and His ultimate plan and purpose for my life, and everyone's.

The first thing I want to say is, thank you!

Thank you for all your support and prayers over this past year. I'm positive they went a long way in allowing me to keep my sanity throughout months in hospital and ups and downs and everything. The power of prayer can't be matched at all. Thank you very much for that.

Thank you to everyone who came out this past week to wave at me as I was supposed to fly over the church building. It didn't work out that way. But we got up eventually, and it was very good.

Thank you also for letting my dad and family have some extra time off to spend time together. It's been very good, and I appreciate it a lot.

Secondly, I want to talk about suffering a bit.

I think I've learned a thing or two about suffering over these past twelve months, and I wonder, what has been accomplished for God's ultimate will through my suffering? If it had just been a "normal year," then life would have continued as normal. But how many opportunities for God would have been missed if I hadn't endured that?

I've learned this past year that it is possible to suffer and go through terrible circumstances with a smile on your face and not have to ask the question "Why me?" God's plan is bigger than all of us. His plans always work out perfectly, according to His will. So why should we waste our time asking "why" when instead we can sit back and just say "Wow!"?

I can keep a smile on my face because I've learned that suffering isn't a punishment from God or a curse from Satan. Instead, I've learned that my suffering is a rare opportunity from God to showcase how awesome He really is.

While battling leukemia, I have also learned that suffering has a way of connecting people, sometimes in weird circumstances, but the result is usually for the better. These past twelve months, I have met and been helped by many, many incredible people, many people who do not have a relationship with God. I guess I won't really know fully until eternity what impact my story may have had on them. But, if I was able to see a few of these people when I get to heaven, or when they get to heaven, just think of how exciting that is!

My suffering has also connected me to God in ways that only after living through this kind of circumstance would you be able to understand. I hope that somehow, through my suffering, you have been able to be connected to God in a deeper way, too.

A cool thought I just got yesterday while running over this for a final time was that maybe my temporary suffering here on earth has brought others to God, ultimately preventing them from eternal suffering in hell! So that's just, I don't know, a thought I had yesterday.

And finally, to sum up this whole suffering thing, I read a quote a few weeks ago, and here it is: "Our healing begins when we participate in the suffering of God; when we don't avoid it but enter into it, and in the process, enter into the life of God; when we see our pain not as separating us from, but connecting us to our Maker."

Finally, I want to talk about death.

I wonder if you have ever really thought about death. Like, not just a casual crossing your mind or passing thought—everyone's done that. I mean really, really thought about death, because I have a little bit.

I don't mean to brag or sound proud or be boastful or anything, but I'm not afraid to die at all. I'm not worried about my death. I'm not afraid, because I'm a Christian. I know that death just means I move from this life on to an eternal party in heaven. I can say one hundred percent honestly that I am not scared to die, but I'm very excited actually. Just to think that there will be no pain or suffering—just partying and eternal happiness!

My name is written down in heaven! Think about that! "Benjamin David Elliott" *is physically written down in the Book of Eternal Life! If that's not a cool mental image, then I don't know what is!*

Psalm 139:16 says, "All the days ordained for me were written in your book before one of them came to be," *meaning that God was in charge from the day I was born and is equally in charge until the day that I die and He takes me home. So, I don't have to be worried or afraid; I just have to trust Him!*

It says in 1 John 3:2 that when we die, we will be like Jesus. Now, maybe I'm taking this verse a little bit out of context, but just think about this: when Jesus came back to earth, He was able to physically walk through walls. I don't know, I just think that's kind of cool!

So, yes, God wants us to have a long life on earth and enjoy ourselves, but just think of how incredible eternity will be! We as Christians should not be scared of death. Instead, we should look forward with hope to an amazing eternal life in heaven.

Ultimately, it all comes down to our relationship with Jesus. It's not about religion; it's about a personal relationship with Jesus Christ.

So, I guess the bottom line and big question is this: are you just a religious person, or do you have a personal relationship with Jesus? Is your name written down in the Book of Eternal Life? If it's not, you should definitely take some time out of your day to think about how awesome eternity can and will be if it's spent with God in heaven! Then I can see you there, and we can party forever!

My ultimate prayer is that God's will, will be done and that everyone will be okay with that, whether that's living for ninety more years or going to see Him very, very soon. The truth is, as a Christian it doesn't really matter, because there is no bad option. It's a win-win either way.

Here is a final verse that I'm not going to read. You have to look it up in the Bible if you care enough. It's just a verse that has kept me going throughout this past year. God takes care of every single detail in our lives—very, very, very specific details. And I think that's cool, too! Thinking that someone cares that much about me, and knows so much about me, is a very humbling thought. So, I'll leave you with Matthew 10:30.

Thank you again very much for your prayers.[2]

---

[2] Ben's sermon can be viewed on YouTube. Just search for "Ben Elliott, Stratford."

• • •

Prayer Journal Entry
Sunday, August 9, 2009

We made an appearance at church this morning. Ben had a message he wanted to deliver to our church family. It was absolutely *amazing…* in *every* way. The fact that he was even able to stand for those ten minutes was a miracle in and of itself! It was the most profound example of Your power being perfected in weakness that I have ever witnessed! And then to hear what he had to say. Wow! We got it on video, which will definitely be a keeper!

• • •

To say that many were blessed and impacted deeply as a result of Ben's response to God's nudging would be an understatement. Many said it was the best sermon they'd ever heard.

When we got home, there was a huge thunderstorm outside. The sky was blacker than I have ever seen in daytime hours. We helped Ben onto the front porch so we could watch as the rain began to pelt down. When the wind picked up, we moved back inside. Ben flopped onto the couch in the most satisfied way. He had a look of deep resolve as if to say, "It is finished."

Recalling, once again, the conversation that Ben and I had shared shortly after his diagnosis about finding purpose, it occurred to me that he had found it! Ben knew he had lived, suffered, and was preparing to die to bring glory to his personal Lord and Savior, Jesus Christ—and he wasn't ashamed to say so!

After spending a few more hours at home, we headed back to the hospital. It was hard to imagine that we had now lived almost a complete year of organized chaos, orchestrating family visits, moving in and out of the hospital, living two lives (one at home and one in the hospital), making arrangements for our kids, and dealing with ups and downs and blow after blow. Now, it was just a matter of time before we would say goodbye to our precious son.

Later that day, when we began to more seriously discuss the potential of bringing Ben home to spend his final days, I became very agitated. It was something not many ALL (Acute Lymphoblastic Leukemia) patients have the opportunity to do, and I wasn't thrilled about the prospect of being in the minority. For one, it meant being faced with the potential of medical crises beyond our capability. Secondly, it meant juggling full-time responsibility of Ben's healthcare with family matters and the potential of well-intentioned people dropping by more regularly.

121

The Ben Ripple

Everything inside me feared, even rebelled against, bringing him home. My inner conflict was raging. I was terrified of having to watch Ben suffer any more than I already had. Stress and emotions were high between David and me, especially when I walked into Ben's hospital room the next morning to find that David had it all packed up and ready to go.

Desperately looking for support, I took the liberty of expressing some of my concerns and fears to the nurses, and we rallied some of our medical team together. However, they knew better than to take sides. Instead, they wisely and sympathetically advised me to carry on the way I had been doing… taking things one day at a time… enjoying life along the way and everything that goes with that… not wishing anything away.

I knew that the final decision had to be Ben's, and it was obvious that he wanted to spend his last days in the comfort of his own bed, surrounded by the sights and sounds of home. What was I to do but get out of the way and let God be God, entrusting Ben one more time into His capable, loving, and nail-scarred hands?

• • •

Prayer for Benjamin Elliott
Tuesday, August 11, 2009
We felt it would have been unwise to even consider bringing Ben home without first taking time to weigh the pros and cons. There has been much to consider, arrange, and get our hearts and minds around in order to make it happen.

From the outside, some might think that we're bringing Ben home to die. We, however, look at it as bringing him home to *live*. As much as we've felt cared for beyond the call of duty and we've appreciated the love and support of our hospital family, whom we will miss inexpressibly, as of late it's become an "existence" for Ben. It's also been difficult for our family to be apart, and if there's a time for us to all be together in one place, it's now.

Pray that Ben will be able to enjoy all he can in these upcoming days here at home. Pray that God will continue to give us some lasting family memories. And, of course, pray that God will continue to be glorified as we live out the remaining time for us to be together here on earth.

Believing that God's perfect love will cast out all fear,
Lisa (Mom)

• • •

From all appearances, anyone reading my Facebook updates would have concluded that all was well with my soul regarding the decision to bring Ben home.

However, Ben's VON nurse Ruth-Ann, having worked alongside us anytime Ben was at home, easily picked up on my apprehensions and spoke to me privately at her first opportunity. After I tearfully stated my case, she lovingly shared her experience caring for her own mother at home in her dying days. She assured me that I wouldn't have any regrets.

Finally, she told me that my main responsibility was to love Ben, and she was confident that I would do that well. My sister-in-law, too, had told me that she was praying I would experience some unforgettable moments with Ben to add to my heart-treasury. I clung to every reassurance I could get and slowly began to feel God's love casting out my fears.

• • •

Prayer for Benjamin Elliott
Saturday, August 15, 2009
It has been twenty-eight days since Ben found out that his final round of chemo did not work. His main oncologist (who had been on holidays for two weeks) told Ben this past Monday that he was very surprised to see him. He hadn't expected Ben to live two more weeks. So, we thank God for each day with Ben.

However, Ben's body continues to grow weaker. He can only walk (shuffle) a couple of feet before he needs to sit down to catch his breath. He is beginning to bruise over various parts of his body. Both of his eyes are now blurry. His headache, nausea, and vomiting continue to plague him. His fever is relentless. His "outer man" is decaying day by day.

But in spite of all this, his inner man continues to thrive. He remains very positive and joyful! Just a couple of nights ago, we moved his bed up from the basement to the living room. (The nine stairs to his bedroom are now more than he can handle.) His bed is set up right in front of our living room window. We joked with him that we were going to charge $25 a person to come look at him through our front window. Ben responded to our teasing by suggesting we put a note on the window reading, "PLEASE DO NOT BANG ON GLASS!" Praise God for laughter in the midst of tears!

Ben is *very* happy to be home. We have already had some special times as a family, for which we are so grateful. Each moment we have together is an absolute blend of joy and sorrow.

Claiming God's strength for each moment,
Lisa (Mom)

The Ben Ripple

Prayer for Benjamin Elliott
Sunday, August 16, 2009

Allow me to confess to you that I was filled with a very tangible fear at the thought of bringing Ben home. This fear, especially in the first few days of being home, was overwhelmingly paralyzing. In my heart, as much as I know this is Ben's wish and that God will grant me all I need to do to make it happen, I came home feeling not only fearful, but every fathomable relative of fear itself. I feel inadequate, insecure, ill-equipped, highly unprepared, and incredibly alone. When asked what I'm fearful of, I can't quite articulate it other than saying that *everything* about bringing Ben home scares me to the max.

God used someone I love dearly to remind me of a book I had given to her years ago, called *Hinds Feet on High Places*, by Hannah Hurnard. In a nutshell, the storyline is about a main character called "Much Afraid" who is destined to marry "Craven Fear." Her fear so overtakes her that she feels paralyzed to climb to the heights of the mountain with the Shepherd of the hills. Eventually, she responds to the Shepherd's call and begins the ascent... much to her surprise, with two companions called "Sorrow" and "Suffering." (It's a definite must-read!)

My greater fear has been that my fear will blind me to what God still has in store for me to experience and see Him do in our midst... and you can bet that I don't want to miss a thing! I want you to know that after a tearful conversation with my husband, heartfelt prayer, and quality time spent asking God to refocus me on all the beauty of bringing Ben home rather than all that could possibly go wrong, I have woken up today with a complete transformation in my heart, knowing and believing that it is in my weaknesses that God's power is perfected (2 Corinthians 12:9).

God is the great "I Am," the all-sufficient One who will not only transform my weakness, but will transform my fear into love. I have realized anew this morning that all God is expecting me to do is *love* my son in his final days. And with His help and strength, I can do that! It is the most incredibly freeing thing to sweetly surrender our all to the One who *is* All!

I surrender All,

Lisa (Mom)

Prayer for Benjamin Elliott
Monday, August 17, 2009

To say that the past few days have been heart-wrenching and excruciating would be an understatement. Yet we are so glad to have Ben at home, where he desires to be, and to have these moments of private joy and mourning as we keep watch over him every single minute of every single day. He is slowly leaving this home of ours to go to his eternal home where his heavenly Father awaits his arrival and has, in fact, been preparing a place for him from the beginning of time.

We've spent time each day, oftentimes at Ben's initiative, going out to the backyard garden swing where he can sit comfortably and enjoy the birds, fresh air, and warm gentle breeze that God's blessed us with these past few days.

On Friday night, he wanted to invite some of his close buddies over to sit and hang out in the backyard with him for a while. It was a mixed blessing to have them all here, laughing and carrying on. Ben took a notion to head down to the Avon River to feed the ducks just a couple of nights ago. It was going great until the swans took a notion to join our adventure!

David heard recently that a person is never truer to himself than in his last days. Although he is still conscious, and somewhat aware of his surroundings, it is very evident that Ben spends most of his time dreaming of a better place. In his dreams, he laughs and smiles and teases and calculates as he always has… and still gets disgusted with me, raising his eyebrows and rolling his eyes even with his eyes closed as if to say, "Ah, Mom!" He continues to say "thank you" for the simplest things, and he engages in conversation as he becomes more aware—I'm sure just to prove to us all that he's still as determined as ever. He talks almost nonstop in his dream-state about all the things that have always been near and dear to his heart—mainly his family and his girlfriend—and often throughout the day he asks for the roll call, taking inventory of everyone's whereabouts over and over again.

A close second to those he loves, his mind seems to be forever on food of some sort. Maybe it's all the months he's spent watching the Food Network! Yesterday he was very delicately eating cream puffs in his dreams, and it was a sad delight to watch him enjoy every bite. Heavenly delights, to say the least.

Today he told us out of his dream-state that there was an incredible smorgasbord. We couldn't help but wonder if he was getting a glimpse of the great banquet table being set for those invited to the wedding feast of the Lamb referred to in the book of Revelation.

Please continue to pray that God will keep Ben comfortable. We thank Him that Ben is not suffering, even though his breathing is much shallower and he is increasingly weak. Pray for wisdom as we make some tough decisions in the days to come. Pray that when the time comes for him to leave us, God will simply close his eyes and embrace him in his Fatherly arms. Pray for our other three children, and for Sarah, as they come to terms with all that is unfolding before our eyes. And pray that God will enable us to care for Ben with every breath he breathes.

There will be a day when there will be no more tears, but rather, as Ben would say, "just one eternal *party!*"

Lisa (Mom)

Prayer for Benjamin Elliott

Tuesday, August 18, 2009

I recently heard, via my brother, from a fellow sojourner whom I've never met, something that rings in my heart so loudly that I couldn't keep it to myself. He said, "All year I've been praying for a miracle for Ben. I just realized that the miracle *is* Ben."

This sentiment has been reinforced through reading the multitude of responses from those people whose lives have been impacted in some way by Ben throughout his nineteen years. Ben truly *is* the miracle.

Lisa (Mom)

• • •

We all continued to hope for the best while preparing for the worst. But no matter how much one prepares for the end, nothing can fully prepare you for it.

I had not left Ben alone throughout our journey. I was fully aware that his language of love was "time," so I considered it my gift to him. On August 18, 2009, I was more impressed than ever not to stray far from his side. I did all I could to keep him comfortable throughout the day and cherished every single minute as I massaged his back that afternoon and into the evening. At midnight, his breathing became labored. We held hands, and I looked into his eyes and said, "Ben, if I could breathe for you, I would."

These were my last words to him before he slipped away.

Ben was finally home.

• • •

Prayer for Benjamin Elliott
Wednesday, August 19, 2009

In John 12:24, Jesus declares, *"The truth is, a kernel of wheat must be planted in the soil. Unless it dies it will be alone—a single seed. But its death will produce many new kernels—a plentiful harvest of new lives"* (NLT).

Early this morning, God chose to take the "kernel" of our beloved son. We pray and believe that Ben's death will, indeed, produce *many* new kernels, a harvest of souls for Jesus.

Ben passed away around 12:30 this morning. He was not feeling well at all yesterday. As the evening progressed, his breathing continued to become shallower and labored. It was quite difficult at the end, but God's grace was sufficient, and Ben passed away quickly.

Our hearts are absolutely broken at the loss of our boy, but we do not grieve as those who have no hope. We are already looking forward to and longing for that wonderful reunion day when we will once again embrace our Ben.

In the meantime, we have been given a sacred trust. Ben ran the race for Jesus so courageously and faithfully. He has now passed the baton on to us and wants us to finish what he started. Please pray for us, specifically as we plan and prepare the details for Ben's funeral. We believe that great things will be accomplished as we honor our son and, more importantly, honor his Lord and Savior.

Please pray that the soil of people's hearts will be fallow, broken, and open to the simple seed of the good news about Jesus. The "kernel of wheat" must be planted and die in order to produce much fruit. We are believing God for an abundant harvest!

Lisa (Mom)

CHAPTER 11

THE

RIPPLE

In Ben's final days, David and I thought it would be a good idea to ask those who had so faithfully sojourned and prayed with us to send notes to express how Ben and our family's journey have impacted their own lives. Our intent was to read to Ben as many of these responses as we could, in hopes that they would bring comfort and give him the assurance that neither his life nor his death was in vain. The response was absolutely overwhelming and continued to roll in even after his passing!

We read a number of the responses to Ben, until he could no longer take them all in. Initially, that made me very sad. However, I began to slowly understand. It would seem that he got to a place where he could no longer receive praise here on earth, but rather he was readying himself for his Heavenly Father's praise.

My prayer became that once Ben arrived through heaven's gates, God would take him up on His Fatherly lap and read him the rest, saying, "Well done, my good and faithful servant."

The following are excerpts of *some* of the notes we received.

———————

The first thing Ben taught me was a little game called "Twenty Questions." So, in keeping with the game, let me begin!

1) Is it an object? No.

2) Is it a human? Yes.

3) Is it a male? Yes.

4) Does this person possess an amazing wit and sense of humor? Yes.

5) Is he sweet? Definitely.

6) Was he raised by parents that you aspire to be like one day? Yes.

7) Does he show a sincere love and respect for his family? Yes.

8) Is he humble, sincere, and one of the bravest people you know? Yes.

9) Does he ask little of others? Yes.

10) Does he have the cutest girlfriend ever? I'd say that's a definite!

11) Is this person wise beyond his years? Yes.

12) Does he look remarkably like Matthew Fox from *Lost*? Yes!

13) Does simply being around him make you smile? Yes.

14) Is he a master jewelry maker? I have proof that he is!

15) Does this person possess qualities you wish you had? Yes.

16) Does this person love Bruce Springsteen? I think he secretly does! LOL.

17) Has this person touched the lives of many people? Yes! Without even meaning to.

18) Does he mean something to you? More than he knows.

19) Will you think of God and the power of faith differently from this point of your life on because of him? Definitely.

20) Has this person changed your life? Yes!

Megan, Oncology Nurse (London, Ontario)

———————

I really wanted to let Ben know how he has helped me change throughout this past year. Ben, you have shown such strength and courage, and you take life head-on. You have shown me that the little disappointments and bad days I have can be dealt with in two ways, the first being to let rough times affect me in the worst way possible. The second, or what I like to call "the Benspective" (mix of *Ben* and *perspective*, in case no one caught that), is not to complain about the pain I'm going through, but use my own trials to build others up.

The Benspective means displaying godly characteristics in times when no one can see the bright side to things. The Benspective is an amazing attitude towards life that even when I'm feeling so alone and down, I can still smile, knowing that God is in control of all things in heaven and here below.

Ben, you helped me realize just how much God provides and cares. Sometimes His answer to prayer is "no," and that's okay, because it just shows us that

God has something so much better and so much more amazing than we could ever hope or pray for.

Taryn (Alberta)

Ben, it has been months since I was first on Facebook searching for a different Ben Elliott. I came across your group. I'm twenty-three and a neuro nurse in the state of Indiana. I have been working for six months in a unit where young men and women our age die from horrible accidents. I'm a new nurse and have really struggled working there, watching families and friends weep over their loved ones. Yet the messages sent by your mom have kept me going. They remind me that God orders our steps sometimes in very different directions, but God's steps are always the best steps.

It is hard to understand why bad things happen to good people, especially to God's people. Yet, I have to admit, Ben, I'm a little jealous of you. I know it sounds crazy but, you see, Ben, you have experienced Christ in a way that most never get to experience. Thank you, Ben, for being faithful. Your faithfulness has brought to light my pride. Know that a young heart has wept for you and your family today. We do not know each other, but we will meet soon enough. I look forward to it.

Wesley (Indiana)

Ben, your journey has taken me in the past twelve months to a place I have run from for many years. I remember you as a blond-haired, blue-eyed little guy running through the foyer of the church your parents ministered in when I was a teenager. For some strange (and uniquely Facebook) reason, I reconnected with your family and your story and have cried tears with every email since. Tears for your strength. Tears for your suffering. Tears as I fought to pray to a God who had seemingly disappeared from my life ages ago.

Usually, when chaos and struggles come my way, I hide, run, or dive for seeming shelter. Your life (not just a story) has made me question God in ways I haven't in years. For me, it is a scary but ultimately good thing. At first, receiving your mom's emails was more about gossip than genuine care. Boy, was I wrong! I'm not sure I have all my answers (or that they are even coming in the time and fashion I desire), but I have started to pray again in earnest for things I didn't even know were my deepest desires.

The Ben Ripple

I see your courage, your mother's words of sustaining hope, and your family's commitment to be by you as evidence that God is still out there, even if not fully evident to me yet. I pray for the journey you are on to be fully revealed to all those who need God's message from it and to be a complete blessing to those travelling with you. You've certainly brought me to a place I couldn't have imagined.

Suzanne

Witnessing from a distance the struggles of the last year and seeing Ben's constant strength and positive attitude has put a lot of things in perspective for me. I realized that I spent a lot of my life living in fear, being scared to try new things and saying, "Oh, I can do that tomorrow." I have changed my outlook. I have started to say "yes" more, and the experiences I've had are amazing. I realize that time with friends and family is precious, and I've learned to appreciate every moment. I think the biggest thing Ben has taught me is to take everything in stride, and that God will never give me more than I can handle. If I just lean on Him, He will carry me through it. I think I had forgotten that.

Andrea (Alberta)

I am a missionary who works in Brazil. We have heard about Ben and prayed for him during our year on furlough. I am about as close to sixty as Ben is to twenty, but he has gone before me. I am at a time of life where I occasionally wonder about death, nursing homes, and final times. Watching God walking with Ben and your family has been another reminder that I don't need to worry. God is in the business of walking with us every inch of the way, and maybe especially in the last inches.

Ben, we are glad for your courage and for all you and your family have learned this last year, although we would love to change things even now. You have walked with our Lord Jesus in a terrible valley but have shown, one more time, that as Christians, we always have Him at our side.

John (Brazil)

Yes, yes, yes, Ben's story has impacted my life and the lives of those I retell it to. I have laughed and cried as I've read your updates. I have wondered how

I would handle a similar situation. I have seen by the example of your family that God's grace *is* enough. I have prayed that God would work a miracle in Ben's body. I have been astonished at the depth of Ben's faith, and I have been reminded once again that it's in adversity that we learn and grow and truly trust in God. I have been reminded of the certainty of heaven.

Gwen (Ontario)

Lisa, you and your family have inspired me. Your views, beliefs, and words make me want to become a better person. I feel as though reading all your messages, and hearing the way Ben handled his situation so strongly, has made me do some serious soul-searching, has made me believe again and follow my faith once more. I've never admitted this to anyone, but recently I began to lose my faith in God and started to doubt my purpose. Reading your amazing and heart-filled daily messages brought me back to where I should have been all along. Ben's story has touched my heart in so many ways.

Paige (Stratford, Ontario)

I feel that Ben's courage and inspiration have really helped me with my own health issues with cystic fibrosis and have helped me realize that death should not be feared.

Danielle (London, Ontario)

Oh, how I miss you guys! I miss everything about you guys... your laughter... your smiles... your positive attitude... your faith... and your altogether closeness as a family!

Ben, I am so happy that I got to meet you. Please know, Ben, that you made a very big impact on my life. Every now and then we get the privilege to meet that one special patient whom we never forget and always talk about—for me, you are that one! Thank you for making me appreciate life to every extent and making me thankful for every day that I spend with my family.

Malinda, Oncology Nurse (London, Ontario)

―――――――――

It's strange, because although I've never met you or your family, I feel connected to you. Your testimony has made me recognize what's important in life—and that's living for God and trusting in Him. That's what matters. This world is so temporary for all of us, but eternity with our precious Lord is forever.

Up until a few months ago, I wasn't relying on God in a number of areas in my life… I often felt depressed by situations and didn't share my faith with others. But now, I'm trying to have a close personal relationship with God, and I've been feeling more at peace than I have for a long time. I feel that the Lord is showing me things that I couldn't understand or see before, and it's starting to change me. Now, when I'm with my co-workers and non-Christian friends, I feel the urge to share my faith with them.

Julie

―――――――――

Ben's story is one I hold close to my heart at all times. I am not, nor have I ever been, deeply religious. It is Ben's perseverance and commitment to sustaining a joyful and awe-inspiring demeanor throughout all the trials that allows me to persevere through my own, comparably trivial, trials. For years, I've struggled with depression and anxiety.

Ben and I met on the first day of school in eighth grade, and I was incredibly nervous. I was starting from scratch, having attended Montessori school up until then. Ben's sense of humor and friendliness helped me want to come to class every day.

Ben and I were never terribly close friends, but we always made a point of saying hi in the halls. I don't think I can recall a time when he didn't have a smile on his face. He was one of the people I envied. Life seemed so simple for him. My life seemed like a never-ending battle with family, friends, but most of all—myself. When I heard about Ben's illness, I realized how simplicity is the least of our worries in this life, and that complications show us who we really are.

Throughout the past few months, I've had a few trying tests of will and character. I've struggled to want to get up in the morning, but your posts, Lisa, have given me a window into a world that gives me the courage to face every day with a sense of humor and commitment to make it through.

So thank you.

Ben, you are indeed the miracle. I thank you for showing me that regardless of the battles we face in life, it is always possible to keep on keeping on, with a smile. I thank you.

Emilia (Stratford, Ontario)

Ben's courage and faith have really opened my eyes to the reality of a relationship with Jesus… I have often asked myself what difference Jesus has made, really, in our lives, as they have been so good and often, for lack of a better word, easy.

Jeff (Ottawa, Ontario)

Thank you, Ben and family, for showing me true faith in action. What an example you have set! One of my favorite chapters in the Bible is the faith chapter in Hebrews. When I read it now, I'll be slipping the Elliott family in there. "By faith, when Ben Elliott was diagnosed with leukemia, neither he nor his family asked why, but kept their eyes on Christ and His reward." I have no doubt that everyone who has come in contact with you, Ben, has seen your love of Jesus and your trust in Him.

Tanya (Belleville, Ontario)

Hey there, Ben. I have been wrestling with words to write to you about how much your testimony of your rock solid and deep-rooted faith in Christ Jesus has reached into my personal life this past year and cemented itself there. God has used you in extraordinary ways.

I believe that people find in you something worth imitating. Without us knowing it, God has used you to give my husband fresh courage for his difficult journey ahead. Scripture teaches us that our lives are like open books read by all. How I see Christ and the hope of glory in you.

Donna

Your lives have touched our floor at the hospital in a very special way. If I may say so, I think that you and your family represent true hope. Maybe, without people truly being conscious of that, they gravitate to you because of what you live out… it is refreshing, and it is outside the norm.

Heidi, Oncology Nurse (London, Ontario)

As our own family goes through the challenges of leukemia with my five-year-old niece, your updates and insights into the Word have been a regular encouragement to me and everyone who reads them. To read about Ben's courage and humor through it all has been so uplifting in keeping the trials of life in perspective. We don't laugh at the trials but delight that the Lord is in control during them, prompting us that "His grace is sufficient for us."

Bryan (Cambridge, Ontario)

Over the past year, my family and I have shared your journey as a family and have laughed, wept, and prayed for you as you've shared with our family all the trials you have endured. Recently Ben's sermon, shared through Facebook, touched me in a very profound way. I was moved to tears as I read the gospel message proclaimed so clearly by Ben to the people of the Church. God's plan is so far outside our comprehension, and much of life feels unfair. But through all his struggles, Ben's positive attitude and desire to help others has reminded me again of the importance of living each day in God's will.

Ron (Mississauga, Ontario)

"Some people come into our lives and quickly go. Some stay for a while and leave footprints on our hearts, and we are never, ever the same." Your story of a wonderful faith and positive attitude, Ben, is an inspiration to all who have heard it, and you have left many footprints on many hearts. Thank you for encouraging the rest of us to keep on believing, even in the midst of life's difficulties!

Nancy (Kitchener, Ontario)

I write to you with tears streaming down my face. I haven't ever met a family with the faith and willingness to share it with so many people, in spite of the anguish you have all had to endure and walk through. I watched the group on Facebook grow, and every time there were new members, I prayed for the non-believers to be inspired and saved. At work, I share your writings with co-workers so that they may also know our Jesus. I prayed that you, Ben, would somehow be able to share; you did, yesterday. I printed off that email and circulated it around the office. I know that these women I work with will have changed lives. That Facebook group isn't by accident. You know every heart of each member and know the ones that are in need of salvation. Bring more to the site so that they can also be ministered to, so Ben's journey will serve a beautiful purpose.

Marg (Mitchell, Ontario)

I was diagnosed with cancer in February of this year. It was the most frightening and uncertain time of our family's life. As we processed this news, it was hard not to slip into a terrible mental place. God's goodness and faithfulness always shone through the dark moments. His glory was only magnified.

I want to thank Ben for his faith and courage. When I wanted to feel defeated and like I couldn't go on, your updates would come through. I have sat countless times in front of the computer, crying and praying for your family, pouring my heart out to God, praying that our response would be like your response to trials, that of Christ.

You may never realize how far-reaching your testimony has gone and continues to go. My nurse (also a nurse of Ben's) shared with us how your faith has been the springboard for her faith to grow larger than it has ever been! Praise God!

Melissa (Stratford, Ontario)

I've never met you, but I have read every single update that your mother has written, and it always knocks me to my knees and just breaks my heart. I've been dealing with trying to figure out why bad things happen to good people. I still don't know the answer to that one, but your story has been a huge wakeup call in my life. I want the joy and peace that you have. I want to be on fire for God!

Jennifer

Words cannot even express the magnitude of the lessons Ben's life has taught me, the biggest of which is "Fear not." Ben's story has truly changed my life and my perspective on things. I can't thank you enough for letting us into his world (and yours) this past year. You have altered the life paths of multitudes of people, mine included. From the bottom of my heart, I thank you.

Pamela (Brantford, Ontario)

Ben's story has made me think, a lot, about suffering.

I sometimes struggle and ask why things happen to me. But now I'm sure I won't say that anymore, and instead try to see how my suffering can bring me closer to God and what lessons He wants me to learn.

I have been praying for Ben, and so has our church here in Portugal (a little town called Oliveira do Hospital). Ben's story has helped me share with my friend, who may have a brain tumor, how God has been so good to you in spite of the situation.

Paula Marques (Portugal)

P.S. May I ask your permission to translate Ben's testimony at your church last Sunday, to share with our church here in Portugal.

Over the past few months, I have read your posts. They have been inspirational. It is easy to talk about faith when everything is going great, but in the midst of the battle, to be able to focus on God… that is amazing. We now know that He is the God of the mountain as well as the God of the valley.

Reverend Mark

You don't know us personally. I began following Ben's progress and praying, and then my husband also began following Ben's story. This surprised me. My husband had walked away from God thirty years ago. Over the years, he had very gradually come back… but only to the fence, so to speak. And there he sat, on the fence, but as he followed Ben's story and "saw" the faith and courage—and, for want of a better word, serenity—that not only Ben, but all of you, showed, my husband moved gradually off the fence and into Jesus' backyard. He has now, over the past few months and weeks, got on speaking terms with God again. I put a lot of it down to God's somehow using the journey that Ben and all of you have been on. Thank you.

Diana

Ben's life (and your Facebook updates) has given me a renewed sense of passion to see others come to faith in Jesus. In many ways, I've been taking my life and my time on this earth for granted, but God has taught me afresh, through Ben, to live my life to the fullest for Christ and not to waste a day worrying about what doesn't matter for eternity. For that, I will be eternally grateful, and when I see Ben in heaven, I can't wait to thank him!

I've also struggled, since seminary really, with the problem of evil in this world, and I'd often find myself asking God, "Why?" I knew the theological answers and could recite them without problem, but after reading Ben's talk a couple of weeks ago, I no longer find myself asking "Why?"… only saying "Wow!"

Mark (London, Ontario)

P.S. "Benspective" will be a new regular word in my vocabulary! I think whoever wrote that letter to Ben and your family will have to submit it to Oxford to have it included in their dictionary.

I'm one of the people who never had the privilege of meeting Ben but felt like I knew him because I've been praying for him, and the rest of you, for over a year now. Being able to tell Ben's story was one way to communicate the reality of God in a person's life without preaching. Ben's journey and your reaction to it have inspired me greatly, and being able to tell it to others who are wondering if God is real and worth seeking has been a blessing to me.

Faith (London, Ontario)

You don't know me, but I've been praying for you for a long time. I never once doubted that God would pull through and heal your body. But then on Wednesday, that hope died with you. I'll admit I cried. You were my age. You wanted the career I'm studying for. You wanted the future that I have the chance to have. And you deserve it far more than I do. So I was sad, because even being a Christian for many, many years, I didn't understand why God would take such a precious person home like that. I went to your funeral on Sunday. I drove four hours and sat there with the other thousand people and just expected it to be a service about wondering why you had to go.

Boy, was I in for a real treat. Not only was your family smiling, but they were laughing! Of all the things to do at a funeral! I knew instantly that this funeral wasn't going to be like anything I'd been to before. Sarah got me crying first, because she didn't cry, and I know how much she loved you. So I was confused. Still.

Then your mom. She cried, but she laughed, too. I know that a Christian funeral is more like a celebration of life, but I've really only been to funerals for old people who have had their time and they've lived. But not you. You didn't get to live to be eighty and then die of old age. So I stayed confused as to why I was crying more than them. Turns out you are a funny guy. Your humor came out all through that funeral service. So did your passion, love, and devotion for a God who let you get sick and took you home to be with Him.

Don't worry, I didn't stay confused forever. You made it very clear that your purpose here on earth wasn't to live till you were eighty and die of old age. God already used you, your family, and your leukemia to touch thousands of people, Ben. I pray that one day you will see that.

I know you wanted to go into nursing. Well, in two and a half weeks I start my nursing education at McMaster University. I know it's not much, but I don't know what else to do for you, so I want to dedicate my nursing career to you, Ben Elliott. Because I know that you would have been the best nurse ever. You would have glorified Christ in every single action, told every single patient about the Father's perfect gift and abounding love. I know you would have done that. And I want to do that.

I know you don't know me, but your story and courage have encouraged me to make nursing about more than I ever thought it was before. Yes, I love people, and I want to help them, but I never would have been as good as you. But I'm going to try real hard, because you deserve that much.

Anyway, Ben, thank you. I get it. I'm not confused anymore. Because you've done everything you can down here, and now it's up to us to let your name live on in our lives as inspiration for others, too. I'm inspired. And in four years, if I pass everything, we'll both have a degree.

Carolyn (Huntsville, Ontario)

If one thing is for sure, you have taught me to believe in something beyond us, something that has the power to predict or teach others different things without physically being here with us, but spiritually and emotionally. Ben, you have always encouraged me to have faith, and over the past year I have started praying and believing in God. You are one of those reasons why I took the courage to have faith. So, I'd like to thank you for that. You have been such an inspiration to so many, but especially me.

Cassy (Stratford, Ontario)

Ben, I want you to know that, with the help of Josh, I am starting a golf tournament in your name. It will run yearly, and all of the money that is raised is going toward cancer research.

Jacobus (Stratford, Ontario)

I was thinking today about the conversations we had this time last year about you maybe thinking about becoming a student leader at youth instead of not coming to youth at all. The reason I talked to you about considering a leadership position is that I saw something in you that made me think you could be used of God in interesting ways.

Ben, the way in which you have fought this fight has only strengthened my thoughts that you are one awesome guy. You have fought this battle with grace and perseverance.

Donna (Stratford, Ontario)

Over the past two years, I lost a lot of the faith that I used to have, and I think a part of me was angry. But you and your family have given me hope again in the Lord and in prayer.

Katie (Stratford, Ontario)

Ben's testimony has certainly challenged many people to consider what they really live for. His life and witness have been used by us as pastors in sermons, as well as sharing with people on an individual basis. Ben has witnessed to more people than he will ever realize, at least on this side of eternity.

Bill (Cobourg, Ontario)

You do not know me, because we have never met. My son was in Mrs. Van Essen's class this past year. I want you to know how much you are in our hearts even tonight. I can't sleep, and I am thinking of you, your courage, and the great blessing that you are. You are holding on to Jesus in the toughest of circumstances. That is courage. My son has been touched by you. Our family prays for you.

You are fulfilling *everything* that He has called all His people to do. To love

Him. Thank you. There is something bigger about you. A gift God has given you, Ben. I feel that you are being used by God from right where you are. You may never know how you have impacted the people that you have, but you are a warrior in faith. A statement and a testimony.

Trevor (Stratford, Ontario)

This past year, I have had the opportunity to speak to many people—both believers and non-believers—regarding your illness. Your illness has allowed me to open the door to share with others your incredible love, trust, faith, strength, and commitment to our heavenly Father. I have also talked to them regarding eternal life, and if they have ever thought about what will happen to them when they die.

Gail (Stratford, Ontario)

My name is Stephanie, and I have been forwarded your messages over the past few months. Your faith, courage, and transparency have inspired me more than I can say. I'm sure you know by now that God is using you to reach hearts and lives far outside of your normal sphere of influence.

Ben, I just want you to know that one of the greatest fears of my life has always been of death. Your courage, your obvious love for God, and your rock-solid faith in His goodness through this ordeal have encouraged my heart and eased some of those fears. You and your family have shown so many of us what faith looks like when it hits the whitewater rapids of life. Can I tell you that your faith is making Him look oh so very wonderful? It causes me to rejoice in His greatness and builds my confidence in His commitment to walk through the troubled waters with us.

Steph (Sarnia, Ontario)

After eleven years of nursing in oncology, I feel I have somewhat distanced myself from my patients so that I don't "get close." It's hard to get to know someone and their families and have to say goodbye so often. I'm so glad I got to meet Ben and the whole family. It was just too easy to share stories and many, many laughs! I'm glad I could lift my protective shield away.

From getting to know your family, I have learned that having a strong faith in God is what has helped you cope and understand what is going on. I, in my own personal life, always ask the "why," and I really like how Ben has said it's "wasting time, and this is just God's plan." I feel I totally understand this, and it's time to enjoy the present in every way. Thank you all for sharing your lives with me. I will always have a special place in my heart for Ben and his family.

Julie, Oncology Nurse (London, Ontario)

Ben's story of strength, hope, and perseverance is emotionally captivating and encouraging! Hundreds and thousands have been blessed and challenged by his and, indeed, *your* strength as a family! It's a story of ultimate hope—an eternal hope that outweighs what must be overwhelming pain! What is it that provides Ben and the Elliott family with such tremendous hope? Without a doubt, it's God's love and His mercies, which are new every morning!

Dave (Cambridge, Ontario)

Dear Ben,

You and I have never met. I am a missionary to Indonesia. I am a teacher at a seminary and have taught on the theology of suffering, have preached passages on suffering and trials as pure joy… until I read your speech. I think God has just given me the true definition of what it all means. Thank you for teaching me a very significant lesson about being faithful in the midst of suffering.

Edwin (Indonesia)

Greetings from Korea! I have been forwarded your updates through my former church in Canada. When I read how you are connecting with the Lord and receiving grace to overcome by faith, you make me think of Romans 8:37. In all that the Lord has taken you through, He has made you "more than a conqueror, more than victorious through Jesus Christ."

In the Greek New Testament, the phrase "more than conquerors" is one word: *supernike*. *Nike* is the word for "victory, conquer, overcome" and *super* is the word for "more than." Ben, you are a *supernike*! Your triumphant perseverance by receiving grace from the Lord to overcome is a perfect example of what Romans 8:37 is talking about! I look forward to the day when I can meet you and celebrate with you the *supernike* victory of Christ on our behalf.

John (Korea)

———————

Over the past months, I have been reading your Facebook postings. I have been deeply moved by your journey and in your ability to so succinctly and beautifully describe and record it. I would have to say that what you have been sharing seems almost unbelievable—though to you, I'm sure it is all too believable. But what to many would seem a nightmare, you have transformed into an uplifting song of praise to our God.

Thank you, Lisa, for opening up your heart for us to see. Thank you for providing a window into your soul. Thank you for showing us that we can be vulnerable in our struggles and that God can bless others through our vulnerability. Thank you for the knowledge that God will bless us with peace as we approach the finish line of our race of faith here on this earth.

Lynne (Cobourg, Ontario)

———————

I have sat down to write this several times, and each time the magnitude of the situation has left me at a loss for words. I have laughed and cried, prayed, pleaded, accepted, and rejected the reality. Ben has shown me that the illusion of time is that I always think I have an abundance when really each second is a gift that must be used to the fullest, because it is gone all too quickly.

Ben, over the last year you have redefined strength, courage, and perseverance. I told you the last time we spoke that you were the toughest guy I ever knew, and I meant it. You have taken what you have been given and made it glorify God. You are unbelievable, and you have made my life richer for having been able to call you "friend." Thank you.

Mark (Stratford, Ontario)

———————

It has been such a privilege to know you and be a small part of the journey you have all been walking so bravely. As a Christian nurse on C7, I can say that Ben and each of you have made *such* an impact on the nurses. I often hear them commenting on how special your family is and how much they love you guys.

I know that the way you have handled with such grace and peace each new thing that has been thrown at you has made a lasting impact on all of us. Your family is living proof of the hope we have in Christ and the inexpressible joy and peace that comes from putting our trust in Him, and I know that the nurses have taken great notice of this. Thank you for living out your faith so boldly! You have all really challenged me to be bold with sharing my faith with my co-workers and patients as opportunities arise. All of us on C7 really miss you all!

Ben, thanks for always having a smile on your face and for being so funny, kind, humble, and appreciative. Lisa and David, thank you for proclaiming the Truth with every email you have sent out and conversations in the hallway, etc. You have allowed all of us to experience in a small way this huge thing that you are all going through, and you have such a gift of being real and honest about the ups and downs. Thank you to all of you for proclaiming Christ in your actions, attitudes, and words.

Joanna, Oncology Nurse (London, Ontario)

I was in Brazil co-coordinating a team of thirty-five teenagers from the Mennonite Church of Eastern Canada when the news of Ben's unsuccessful remission reached me on Facebook. The next night, I shared with my small group of seven youth the sorrow I felt, but also the joy of being with them and watching all they were experiencing. These seven youth had a wonderful dialogue with me that night about life, death, faith, and choosing to trust that God sees beyond the small piece we see—that God knows the bigger plan we can only imagine. Together, we sat with our questions, and these teens, none of whom know you, prayed for you and for our own places of doubt and belief. We are yet one more place where God has chosen your story to impact and influence the journey of others.

Anne (Brazil)

Praying for Benjamin has brought me face to face with what I truly believe, value, would be willing to give up to God and still praise Him. Reading of Benjamin's towering faith and submission to God drives me to my knees again, asking for forgiveness for having such a small view of God's sovereignty and His promises. This life gets so big and in the way sometimes. We can't see past it on a cloudy day. It takes the strong wind of faith like Benjamin's to clear the skies of forgetfulness and see God's glory and reach towards it.

Lisa, I don't know what to say to pass on to Benjamin except our love and admiration of a young man I have never met, but will someday. Where we can all delicately dine on Divine cream puffs and, indeed, party on and on and on.

Carol (Ontario)

We have grown to love Ben even though we have never met. He is a wonderful young man. His journey has been long and hard, and we honor the integrity with which he has lived it. I have sent many of the excerpts from Facebook to my niece, who is very close to coming to know Jesus. Someday in heaven, when we all meet, I know that she will mention Ben as an important part of why she has come to know Jesus.

Susan (Abbottsford, British Columbia)

Thank you for the incredible updates of your journey. I overheard a conversation between our seven-year-old and our five-year-old last week about dying. Our son asked our daughter if she was afraid to die, to which she responded, "No, are you?" Our son answered, "Nope. Because when I die, I am going to heaven." I know without a doubt that this conversation came from their knowledge of Ben and what he is going through.

Ben's journey has allowed for some great conversations with the kids about when people are sick, about what it means to have "cancer," and about heaven. Our son has said to me on numerous occasions that he wishes he could be sick for a while "for Ben" so Ben could be healthy. Your journey with Ben is a daily reminder that what we have here on earth means nothing and has made us so thankful for our kids and for each other.

Kate (Stratford, Ontario)

Hey Ben, over the past many months I have had the great privilege of sending your mother's prayer requests on behalf of you… sending them on to thousands of people. If a couple of days go by without me sending one out, I get emails asking how you are doing! You'll have no idea, until you reach heaven, how many lives you have touched. Not only that, but I believe that your story will continue to touch lives for the glory of the Lord for years to come. You will meet those in heaven who will say to you, "Oh, you are Ben Elliott, the young man whose life touched mine. Let me tell you how."

Ben, I am excited how God is going to continue to tell your story and use it for His glory. Even though we have never met you, you are loved by me and my family as well as all those touched by a brave soul called Ben. We continue to pray!

Betty (Ontario)

My husband and I have been following your story since we found out about Ben's diagnosis. We are presently searching for a church home but wanted you to know that in every church we visit, the congregation is praying for Ben. That is about twenty-one churches so far. We actually are just enjoying visiting and waiting for the prayer to see if Ben Elliott's name comes up. Thought I had to drop you a line about this so you realize the scope of how many people are truly praying for Ben and your family.

Candice (Ontario)

Ben's story has impacted and inspired me beyond my expectations. A year of teacher's college and hanging out with educators can negatively affect a person's notion of teenagers. For the most part, teens are viewed as dangerous—part-human and part-beast—who, if left unchecked, may destroy the most intricate of plans. I was instructed that the goal was to herd them, much like cattle, towards their almost certainly unwarranted graduation.

For me, the timing of Ben's battle and my becoming more closely acquainted with your teens and young adults—not only Ben but also Natalie, Jacob, Erin, and Sarah—was fortuitous. Their loyalty, perseverance, mettle, and conviction in the face of more adversity than most of us will ever face maintained and invigorated my faith in teenagers. They helped me see the maturity and grace that adults and educators (in particular) rarely acknowledge. Thank you for allowing me a glimpse into your awe-inspiring family.

Andrew (Stratford, Ontario)

Words cannot describe how I feel every time I receive a message about Ben. He truly is a bright light in this world. I am on dialysis and get very sick from time to time, but Ben has taught me where to keep my eyes focused—and that is on *Him*. His Word is such a blessing of hope and encouragement. I have learned things in His Word because of Ben that I never knew or felt before. I am sixty-eight years old and feel such a renewing of the Spirit. Thank you, Ben.

Barbara

The Ben Ripple

You don't know me. Where do I begin to tell you how your journey has impacted me, my family, friends, acquaintances, and many more to come? As Christians, we use the words faith, hope, love, and trust almost daily—and sometimes very loosely. As our family has been intertwined with your family this past year, these words have taken on a new meaning and a far greater depth.

Ben, I think we are the "Why?"! Your story has and will continue to impact all who it is shared with, Ben, because we are relational beings. Empathy brings us all closer together, and through this, your message will send far-reaching ripples out into the pond.

Graine (Barrie, Ontario)

You have encouraged me when I have felt I could not overcome my fear. You, Ben, have the *victory* we all desire.

Carol Ann (Winnipeg, Manitoba)

I have been following your updates across the world in Australia. I may have only been your nurse a couple of times in the beginning days of your diagnosis, but I still feel a strong connection to your entire family, and I thank you for your continuous positive outlook on life.

Keri-Lyn (Australia)

The train ride from Georgetown to Toronto is slightly over an hour. I sit with three other ladies, all mothers with children ranging from age six to twenty-three, and each of us has been touched in different ways by your words, your faith, and your understanding.

Last week, one of the girls woke us up with the following statement: "Where does she get her strength, and why does she continue to thank God? Where is He for her?" We shared things with each other, which brought us closer, but the real message here is that we have been talking about God, on a crowded train, with passion, openness, and honesty more than once a week for weeks!

Now for the best part. Fellow riders who usually sleep, have their own groups, or who we thought were tuned out of our discussion now sit and watch to see if we are going to begin the "discussion." And if we do, they move closer and join in. So a group of four has turned into a group of twelve to fifteen, with each saying how their souls have been awakened, how really blessed they are, and how they are looking at things in a whole new light. Some have actually gone back to church. Others are contemplating reestablishing themselves with a church.

However, the one true fact is that their souls and spirits have been stirred, all because of you sharing with us and placing God unconditionally in your life.

Donna (Toronto, Ontario)

As of late, I have found myself thinking about God and wondering what it is all about, so much as to have bought myself my first Bible. This is a big thing, as I was never brought up knowing anything about religion. If this God and all His teachings give you both the strength to get up every morning and face what must be so incredibly hard, I have to find out more about Him, and so that is what I've been doing. I also think what a comfort it must be to know that there is someone there always watching over you and loving you throughout your life, even when you think you are completely alone.

Michele (Whitby, Ontario)

A sign on the wall of a junior high classroom contained these words: "Experience is the hardest teacher. It gives the test first and then the lesson." Likewise, I know that you and your family have been learning, and continue to learn, the lessons of suffering. You and your family have truly ministered to me (and those I've shared with) as you have courageously, by God's grace, embraced these lessons. Thank you for your faithfulness in not resisting God's divine plans for your life. I have been a witness of the mighty power of God that has been at work within you.

Thank you, Ben, for showing me the kind of endurance and patience that is eager to trust God and learn lessons His sovereign purpose desires us (me) to learn. It is that very trust that has covered you and those around you to glorify God in the midst of your suffering. We have seen your unwavering trust during the past year and a half as shared on Facebook.

Lisa (Cincinnati, Ohio)

I want to thank you for sharing your heart, for being obedient, and stepping out and being vulnerable to so many of us. You have helped me, as you have already been on the journey that we are just beginning with our ten-year-old son in his diagnosis with ALL. We will be printing Ben's message, along with several other entries, and saving them to share with our son as time moves on. We trust God with the timing of that.

Roseanne (Chatham, Ontario)

My husband is currently a youth pastor, and this weekend we are taking our youth group on a camping retreat. I just wanted to share with you that as we prepare to share the gospel with the group and are praying for a few who are very close to making life-changing decisions, we will be using Ben's journey as a testimony to the power, strength, and love of our Savior and what this does in a life sold out to Him. Thank you for that!

Andrea (Smiths Falls, Ontario)

I only had the honor of meeting Ben once, but I could see right off the bat that he was someone so special. That beautiful smile and the twinkle in his eyes just lit up an otherwise very dull clinic room. I believe that you are showing me a path back to church and God, realizing how much I have missed.

Jane-Ann, Nurse (London, Ontario)

After following your story, how could I possibly feel sorry for myself? I learned from you, Ben, and your family, that we should always honor God through the good times and the bad, and that He will have something good in store for us if we are faithful. So, Ben, I joined another study group at the church and one at the hospital where I work. I am trying to get back on track.

Cynthia (Cobourg, Ontario)

To God be the glory!

CHAPTER 12

Grief
IN THE RAW

When Ben died, our lives changed forever. It was difficult to imagine that things would never be the same again. I was soon to discover that, not unlike the painful journey through my son's illness, grief is also a journey. It is an inevitable and necessary process that you must take in order to find a renewed sense of hope and healing.

I had grown quite attached to those who had so faithfully journeyed with us for an entire year. It was hard to think of saying goodbye to those who had become such an integral part of my life, so it only seemed right to allow them to grieve along with us. Realizing just how far-reaching our story had become, I renamed the Facebook group "The Ben Ripple." My mother's heart found therapy and purpose as I continued to regularly pour my grieving heart out to our fellow sojourners over the next year.

• • •

Tuesday, August 25, 2009: Tears, Talking, and Time

The day after Ben's passing, we got a long-distance call from dear friends of ours who gave us three words of advice in facing the days, months, and years to come. The three words were: "Tears, Talk, and Time."

Believe me when I say that there has been no shortage of tears as we deal with the heartbreak of losing Ben. I said in a previous update that tears are a gift from God Himself. There is healing in tears as we use them to release those feelings that cannot be put into words. No doubt there will be many more to come.

We have spent a lot of time talking about not only this past year, but also memories we've shared over Ben's entire life. We have been surrounded by family and friends and have been given ample opportunity to talk with them about some of the excruciatingly beautiful times that we had with Ben, especially over the last nine days we had him home.

David and I have also spent time talking about what the days ahead could possibly look like from here on.

Time is a healer, and we plan to take the necessary time to grieve our losses and cherish the moments we will spend together discovering our new normal. We realize that we have already been grieving the loss of Ben for this entire year.

We pray that God will open the floodgates of tears as we face the days to come. We pray that God will open many opportunities for us to talk and process His sustaining grace and faithfulness in our lives. And we pray that we will take the necessary time to heal our broken hearts.

Thursday, September 3, 2009: Moments in Time

In one moment we may find ourselves functioning valiantly in a mental task, while the next we find ourselves in an emotionally disabling puddle. In one moment we are seeking to embrace our new normal, while in the next we can hardly imagine what's transpired over the course of this last year. In some moments, a random memory will trigger laughter, which inevitably and, just as spontaneously, turns into heart-wrenching tears.

Having been a year since we began this journey, we find ourselves reliving all the losses we were forced to embrace one by one before losing Ben completely. We are finding at this stage of our grieving that memories do nothing to ease the pain of our loss, but rather only serve to accentuate the gaping hole. We are also dealing with the "never again" moments as we face a future that is void of Ben. He will forever be the empty chair at family gatherings and special events, not to mention at our dinner table.

I am grateful for every single moment granted us.

Lifeline

"Praise be to the God and Father of our Lord Jesus Christ, the Father of compassion and the God of all comfort, who comforts us in all our troubles, so that we can comfort those in any trouble with the comfort we ourselves have received from God. For just as the sufferings of Christ flow over into our lives, so also through Christ our comfort overflows" (2 Corinthians 1:3–5).

Thursday, September 10, 2009: Good Grief!

What does "good grief" really look like?

I've been told many times over that there is no right or wrong way to grieve, that there is no set time frame in which to grieve. There are many faces and phases to grief. I'm discovering this to be true right within our own family. The important thing we continue to do is grant each other permission to grieve our loss of Ben in a good, healthy way. By this I mean that if tears are brimming, we permit them to flow freely. If frustration brews, we permit ourselves to vent it. If we need to let loose and laugh, we give ourselves permission to do just that. If personal space is required, we permit each other the time, space, and solitude that even Jesus permitted Himself to take whenever He went to a lonely place to pray and spend time alone with His Father.

One of the ways we permit ourselves to experience "good" grief is through journaling. We have decided to use it as a family to process our grief, writing down things that we miss about Ben, along with memories and thoughts of Ben as we consider the rest of our lives without him. We pray that as we do so we will truly experience God's grace as we make our way toward healing through "good" grief.

Monday, September 14, 2009: Reentry

I went to church for pretty much the first time in a year last Sunday and found it *extremely* difficult. Although I, the pastor's wife, was a virtual stranger to many who have joined our church family over the time I've been at home caring for Ben, rightly or wrongly I felt I was on display in my grief.

Fortunately, I was given the space I required to just *be* there, and was so grateful that I felt safe enough to claim my own box of Kleenex and sob my way through the entire worship service. We began with a song by Chris Tomlin that has become an anchor for me throughout our journey: "How Can I Keep from Singing Your Praise?" A part of the verse says, "And though the storms may come, I'll keep holding on and to the Rock I'll cling."

Then I was finished off as we belted out Ben's favorite hymn: "Holy, Holy, Holy…Lord God Almighty." Or, as Ben would sing it, "Lord God on my team."

Sunday, September 27, 2009: Grieving Forward

In our grief so far, David and I are listening to and reading a lot of grief material together, the only thing separating us being a box of Kleenex. One of the things we've read from a variety of sources is that when someone loses their parents, they grieve their past. When they lose a spouse, they grieve their present. But when someone loses a child, they grieve their future. This is not meant to in any way minimize but rather to somehow categorize the various types of grief experienced when a loved one dies.

As an aside, have you ever given thought to the fact that there's no word to define a grieving parent? Someone who has lost parents is called an "orphan." Those who have lost spouses are called "widows" or "widowers." But there's no word for someone who has lost a child.

We are finding that it's painful enough to have to face the "never again" moments that, in effect, pull us into the memories of the past, facing what is no longer. Things like not ever being able to hear Ben laugh or see him smile again. We'll never again see him bound in the door full of energy with his contagious zest for life. We will never again have him join us at the dinner table, nor will Ben any longer be around to entertain us with his "Benisms."

However, equally as painful as coming to terms with what we'll never experience again are the "never *will* be" moments. We will never see the look on Ben's beaming face as his bride walks down the aisle, Jacob standing as his best man. We will never be able to see as he welcomes his new baby into the world. We will never be able to include Ben in our family get-togethers and special occasions, watching him as the husband and dad he always longed to be.

As we look ahead into our Benless future, life just doesn't feel right.

What we *are* all looking forward to is the day when we will all be reunited again with Ben in our heavenly home.

We grieve forward but hold fast to our future and eternal hope.

Sunday, October 3, 2009: The Meeting Place

I miss Ben most in my kitchen. That was our meeting place. It's there that for years I've stood in the morning while all the kids get their lunches ready for school, Ben taking pride in his sandwich feasts. It was there that I'd be preparing dinner when they all got home from school.

In most recent years, it's the place where Ben would find me when he burst through the door after school, grabbing a bite before getting ready to run out the door again for work, or coming in famished after volleyball practice. He would often come and help me get things set up for dinner, even coming alongside me to get the meal ready.

He was also known for kicking me out at times to concoct one of his own secret recipes. Ben certainly enjoyed his food, and catering to his cravings was easy because he was so vocal about his likes and dislikes. Among his favorites— homemade pizza, homemade bruschetta, barbecued anything, stir-fry, Thai food, and what would an evening snack be without popcorn. Even in his final week at home, I spent time in the kitchen catering to whatever he asked for… whether or not he could actually eat and enjoy it, which he usually couldn't.

It only makes sense then that the kitchen these days is where I usually find myself at the sink, salting my dishwater or pre-salting food with my tears.

It is very, very sad for each of us to think that we will no longer be able to meet with Ben here on this earth. For now, as each of us carries on in our different directions—whether it's school, church, or varying activities—aside from the obvious family connection, our meeting place is the pain we are all experiencing together.

It occurs to me that, in life, isn't that where all of us meet? There is not a single human being who has not experienced pain of some sort. It also occurred to me in a fresh way that God meets us in our pain at the foot of the cross. The sacrifice of His only Son wasn't simply a demonstration of His love for us, but also proved to be a way that He could enter into our lives. Pain is God's access route into our innermost being. I heard it said again recently, "God whispers to us in our joys, but He shouts to us in our pain" (C. S. Lewis).

Ways to Acknowledge the Elephant in the Room

Almost as painful as people saying the wrong thing to us were those who, not knowing what to say, chose not to say anything at all. We were therefore often left alone… in a room… with an elephant! Here are some helpful hints for ways you can acknowledge the elephant in the room.

- "How are things with you today?"
- "When do you think about your loved one the most?"
- "Are there certain things that trigger your thoughts toward your loved one?"
- "Would you like to talk about your loved one?"
- "I can't imagine the pain you're experiencing."
- "I feel helpless to alleviate your pain."
- "I am praying for you as you deal with your loss."
- "How can I be praying for you?"
- "What overwhelming feeling are you experiencing these days?"
- "What do you miss the most about your loved one?"

Share a memory of the deceased or how he or she impacted your life. Parents and siblings want to know their loved one didn't die in vain, that their life counted for something. Don't be afraid of tears on your own part or on the part of the person who has suffered the loss.

Oftentimes there are no words. If you have nothing to say, just say so! "I don't know what to say."

Tuesday, October 20, 2009: I Do Not Like Green Eggs and Ham!

For the past several days, echoes of one of my favorite children's books by Dr. Seuss, *Green Eggs and Ham*, play over in my head. There is one line in particular, where after being relentlessly offered this dish in various forms, Sam I Am's friend says, "I do not like them here or there. I do not like them *anywhere*!"

As much as we're making the best of things around here and trying to move on with our lives, none of us really likes it… anywhere!

It reminds me of Ben's pill-taking ritual. If there was one thing he detested, it was the countless pills he was prescribed to take numerous times a day. As many times a day as he was required to take them, David or I would put them all into a little bowl and set them at his side along with a glass of water. After sitting for a while, contemplating the order in which he wanted to take them, he picked up his glass of water, took a little swig, and then prepped himself with a few quick breaths before finally putting the first pill into his mouth, taking one more deep breath and swallowing. He did this with each pill for the time it took to consume them all… until next time.

I feel we have a similar ritual these days. In Erin's words, "Every day is the same." We wake up every morning and remind ourselves that Ben is not here. We take a deep breath and swallow that pill. Then, as we're getting breakfast and lunches ready, we look around and realize Ben's not here. But we swallow that pill. We come home from our respective destinations to realize, again, that Ben's not here. Deep breath. We go through our evening, at times flipping through programs that Ben would have liked to watch, *if* he were here. Swallow. We lie in our beds at night and, one more time before attempting to sleep, we try to get our minds around the fact that Ben's not here. And believe me, it's a tough pill to swallow!

We know that Ben would *not* want us moping around, and for the most part I don't feel that we are. But it's still hard to come to terms with the fact that Ben's gone. I think he would be all right with our tears of missing him… unless, of course, they get really out of hand, at which point we can almost hear him say, "All right! Enough already!"

Emotionally it's been a rough week, and as much as we don't like green eggs and ham right now, we'll have to acquire a taste for them. In the meantime, it's good to grieve. It's good to cry. It's good to live life even when it hurts. It's good to trust God.

We breathe deep and swallow one pill at a time.

Lifeline

> "'For I know the plans I have for you,' declares the Lord, 'plans to prosper you and not to harm you, plans to give you hope and a future. Then you will call upon me and come and pray to me, and I will listen to you. You will seek me and find me when you seek me with all your heart'" (Jeremiah 29:11–13).

Wednesday, October 28, 2009: Hindsight is 20/20

As we all know, hindsight is 20/20. It should, therefore, come as no surprise that as we stop and reflect on this last year with 20/20 vision, there comes a clearer view of the reality that took place—and with it a deeper grief.

In our grief, we find ourselves rewinding various events over and over again. We relive everything from the shock of Ben's initial diagnosis to being informed of his high-risk disease to the unraveling events that followed. We also rewind our last week with Ben at home, and more specifically the painful memory of Ben's final hour.

As much as some may try to discourage us from looking back and revisiting all the dark corners, we find it not only therapeutic, but wisely necessary. As difficult as it is, we are grateful to *finally* be able to grieve our losses. With each painful memory comes a deeper sense of respect for Ben and his undefeatable attitude. With each painful memory we are able to, in hindsight, see just how faithfully our God sustained us.

Based upon His Word, God wants us to look back and remember. I've often referred to Lamentations 3:19–23, which says, *"I <u>remember</u> my affliction and my wandering…I well <u>remember</u> them, and my soul is downcast within me. Yet this I call to mind and therefore I have hope: Because of the Lord's great love we are not consumed, for his compassions never fail. They are new every morning; great is your faithfulness"* (emphasis added).

Tuesday, November 3, 2009: Setting the Clocks Back

We celebrated my favorite day of the year just the other day. It's the day we set the clocks back an hour, giving me the extra hour of sleep I annually crave! If only life were like that… just setting the clocks back in time.

The hour that my clock keeps turning back to is Ben's final hour. I've hesitated to put it into writing, and I'm not sure why I feel compelled to tell you about it now. Let me just say that while it was a very sacred time, it was an incredibly horrific time.

At 10:00 p.m., I stepped out of the room to make more tea at Ben's request and walked back in to find Ben, David, and Jacob reminiscing about some of their favorite golf shots until Ben finally said, "Dad, I'm too tired to golf right now."

There was a sad moment of silence before David changed the subject and asked Ben if he was still glad we had brought him home.

"Mmmhmm," he said.

David went on to remind Ben of how stressed out I had been to bring him home. Ben hadn't said more than two words for a couple of days, so it surprised me when he asked, as clear as a bell, "Are you still stressed, Dzum?" *Dzum* was his made-up nickname for me, which also signified that he was *very* with it and was taking in this entire conversation. I was able to assure him, with tears in my eyes, that I was no longer stressed.

As I think about it now, it was Ben's way of making sure *I* was okay. It was likely also his way of making sure that David and I *together* were okay, as there's no doubt that he picked up on the stress between us over bringing him home. Once assured that we were okay, he was okay.

At midnight, Ben's breathing became shallower, and he became very restless. While I went to the phone for some intervention, Ben's time to leave us arrived.

As David describes it, his only words were a question: "Where am I?"

David then replied, "Ben, you're home."

With that, his eyes became very large, and he stared in the direction of his brother, Jacob. Jacob later told David that Ben's stare was so intense that he actually stepped aside, because he felt he was blocking what Ben was trying to look at. Jacob said that perhaps Jesus was coming out of the dining room buffet and hutch to meet Ben and bring him home.

Jacob reminded us of what Ben had said to the church family just ten days earlier, that he thought it was cool that Jesus could walk through walls in His resurrected body. Who knows… Jesus may have done that!

I don't know that our hearts will ever stop longing to set our clocks back to the time when Ben was alive and well here with us. Don't get me wrong; we are rejoicing that Ben is in heaven and more alive and well there than he *ever* was, but it does little to bridge the gap for now, nor does it bring the consolation that I would have thought it would. I'm sure it will come in time, but for now it remains that while heaven has never seemed so real to me, neither has it felt so far away.

It makes me want to set the clocks ahead!

Lifeline

"Now the dwelling of God is with men, and he will live with them. They will be his people, and God himself will be with them and be their God. He will wipe every tear from their eyes. There will be no more death or mourning or crying or pain, for the old order of things has passed away" (Revelation 21:3–4).

Sunday, November 8, 2009: Goin' on a Lion Hunt!

I've been leading children's music from the time I was a child. One of my all-time favorite songs is "Goin' on a Lion Hunt." It's a follow-after-me song with the kids imitating my gestures, so after getting all prepared to venture into the world of the unknown to catch us a lion, we get on our way. Follow after me!

> Goin' on a lion hunt.
> Gonna catch a BIG one.
> I'm not scared!
> And look at these flowers.
> No time to pick 'em.
> Gotta keep moving!
> STOP!
> Do you see what I see?
> It's a great big swamp!
> Can't go around it!
> Can't go over it!
> Can't go under it!
> I guess we gotta go *through* it!

And on the song goes as we encounter one obstacle after another until we finally get to the cave where the lion waits. Believe me, if you've never been on a lion hunt like this before, it's one you don't want to miss!

I think the biggest reality we're facing these days is that there's no way around or under or over what we're experiencing, which leaves us with no other way but to go *through* it!

It's been a very emotional week to go *through*. David and I were already having a cleansing day, so we finally gave in to watching the three DVDs we had made of Ben's viewing and funeral. It was brutal, but very necessary.

Another very significant obstacle we've had to face is that this weekend would have been Ben and Sarah's three-year dating anniversary. This is a significant loss for us, one that we grieve every single day. Ben and Sarah shared a very special relationship.

As always, I can't begin to thank all of you who continue to journey *with* us as we go *through* this difficult time. Thank you for crying with us and hurting with us and praying for us and comforting us simply by sticking *with* us. Thank you for not having answers or advice that would only suit to stifle our grief. Thank you for not attempting to remove the pain or alleviate it or, worse yet, attempt to prevent us from feeling the pain, but thank you for rather allowing us to go *through* it. Thank you for giving us permission to be sad. As much as Ben wasn't big into emotions, I'm pretty sure that he would be okay with our being sad.

Lifeline

"Fear not, for I have redeemed you; I have summoned you by name; you are mine. When you pass *through* the waters, I will be with you; and when you pass *through* the rivers, they will not sweep over you. When you walk *through* the fire, you will not be burned; the flames will not set you ablaze. For I am the Lord, your God, the Holy One of Israel, your Savior" (Isaiah 43:1–3, emphasis added).

Getting THROUGH *Special Occasions*

Birthdays, anniversaries, special occasions, and holidays can prove to be great hurdles to jump after the loss of a loved one. As much as we'd love to skip *over* them, they appear on the calendar and we must go *through* them. The question is *how*? The following are a few ways we dealt with difficult calendar days:

- Take time to grieve your loss.
- Set apart birthdays, anniversaries, and other meaningful days to simply *remember*.
- Read through cards you kept from those who encouraged you through your loved one's illness or death.
- Go down memory lane. Visit places that hold a significant memory of your loved one.
- Sort through memorabilia.
- Make your loved one's favorite meal, snack, or dessert. If you'd like company, invite others who are grieving your loved one to share it with you.
- Connect with others who are also grieving the loss of your loved one or a loved one of their own.
- Give yourself permission to decline invitations to *happy* social gatherings if you're not feeling up to it. Or graciously accept an invitation but tell the person who's invited you that, depending on how you're feeling that day, there is the chance that you may decline at the last moment.
- Do something positive in honor of your loved one. For example, we brought a platter of homemade favorites of Ben's to the hospital.
- Grant yourself the time and space you need surrounding special occasions.
- Write a letter to your loved one.
- Write a letter to others explaining your grief and what they can expect of you through this time.

Wednesday, November 18, 2009: Good Ol' Mountain Air!

David and I were able to get away for a week alone together for the first time since before Ben's diagnosis. We headed for the hills in a very literal way in order to attend a conference nestled in the Blue Ridge Mountains of North Carolina.

One of the main things that came out of our time away was making the encouraging discovery that we are not wallowing, paralyzed, or stuck in our grief. We are able to actually think and plan ahead a little. It is nice to see a bit of the other side of the valley from the mountainside perspective.

There is a certain sense of guilt as we venture forward, however. We feel tension between leaving Ben behind and yet carrying him in a treasured part of our hearts, and knowing that God still wants us to live lives that are rich and full and not void of anything that He has in store for us.

We have been discussing ways to remember Ben—something special that will permit us in a natural way to recognize his absence. We want to find a way, without being morbid, that allows us to keep him a part of us on special occasions or times when we just miss him and need to spend time thinking about him. We found just the thing and purchased an oil wick lantern. Ben would be pleased that it's not some "smelly scented candle," as he would say.

I'm so glad that the God of the mountain is also the God of the valley. It's in the valley that the flowers grow.

Wednesday, December 2, 2009: Christmas Is Coming!

Christmas is coming! I know you all know that, but I'm finding I have to continually remind myself of that these days. Not that I keep forgetting. Au contraire! While signs of Christmas are everywhere I turn, I am bracing myself for all that we'll be noticeably missing this year. Given that Jesus is the reason that I live and not simply the reason for the season, there is a consolation that He will excuse me for wanting to wipe December off my calendar this year.

In our vulnerable state, we can't help but think about last Christmas. I have to believe that the same God who provided Ben with grace—giving him all that he needed to face his year-long battle with leukemia—will also be enough to see us through, especially during this "most wonderful time of the year."

As I've publicly shared our journey, I've become aware of so many others who are experiencing their own grief and who are feeling the same apprehension as they enter into this season to be jolly. I have appreciated the insights into the hearts and lives of several of these hurting souls, not only in order to keep me from feeling sorry for myself, but also to enable us to somehow come alongside them in their sorrow. There is a healing that takes place when we reach beyond ourselves to enter into someone else's pain—and isn't *that* what Christmas is ultimately about?

Emmanuel—God *with* us. As much as God enters into our pain, I've found that He does not impose Himself. He doesn't give advice we're not seeking. However, neither does He always reveal the answers to the questions we're asking. In fact, He may keep totally silent, to the degree that we wonder if He's still there. He certainly doesn't rush us through to the other side of our pain. The fact is, He knows better! He wants us to experience the richness and healing power of His presence *with* us.

So we will venture into this jolly season, albeit with sadness in our hearts, all the while finding strength, comfort, and joy through the One who not only sees and knows and validates our pain, but also provides us with a personal escort.

Sunday, December 13, 2009: What's It All About?

Since last I wrote, I've found myself fighting to keep from spiraling downward into an abyss of meaninglessness. "Vanity of vanities… everything is vanity," Solomon says in Ecclesiastes. Watching the Christmas lights go up in the neighborhood and decorations in the malls, along with the hustle and bustle that peaks at this time of year, seems so empty. I won't be so Scroogish as to call it all humbug; however, it all seems so trivial right now. This has left me with little motivation to join in on all the reindeer games.

The Benspective is reminding me to ensure that the main things are the plain things. At the same time, I need to find joy in the little things. One of the incentives God is using to bring joy into our pain-stricken hearts is Erin. With her prompting, we were able to hunt down a Christmas tree and get it up and decorated. Erin painstakingly and tearfully hung each of Ben's ornaments. She then carefully decorated the entire house, seeking to place things in such a way that mainstay memories would remain dear. Yesterday we baked some of our traditional Christmas goodies with Christmas music blaring… in our PJs! These simple pleasures will hold eternal value in my heart.

I recently came across a quote that Erin has claimed for her own status: "Enjoy the little things in life, for one day you may look back and realize they were the big things."

Comforting Someone Who is Grieving

Not unlike when we were dealing with "the elephant in the room," knowing what to say to someone who has lost a loved one can be a challenge. However, it's not as hard as you might think!

- Listen to me.
- Acknowledge my loss by admitting your inadequacy:
  "I have no words to say."
  "I don't know what I can do to help you in your pain."
  "I'm praying for you while you grieve this incredible loss."
  "I'm so sorry for your loss."
  "I can't imagine how painful this must be."
- Don't be afraid or embarrassed by my tears.
- Use the name of my loved one.
- Acknowledge my other children.
- Express your own emotions or sadness regarding my loved one.
- Assure me that it's not a lack of my faith just because I'm angry or questioning God.
- Listen to me. (Yes, I know I'm repeating myself, but this point is important and I want to make sure you're listening!)
- Help me to realize that each family member will grieve differently.
- Encourage me as a "survivor" of this loss.
- Write me a note to let me know you care.
- Assure me that being strong is not holding back emotions.
- Call me.
- Offer to do specific tasks, but don't be offended if I turn your offer down. Rather, assure me that you'll offer it again some other time.
- Be patient with me.
- Pray for me.
- Listen to me!

Wednesday, December 30, 2009: Surviving Christmas!

We did it! We survived Christmas! As was expected, intermingled with the moments of utter grief and deep sadness were moments of deep joy and new memories that I will treasure in my heart always. David and I were able to conquer and create a "memory room" in order to display all of Ben's earthly treasures. It was a tough job, but we survived the tension and emotion of being surrounded by all of Ben's things that he had carefully "put into order" two weeks before he died. A friend from our church family, gifted at woodworking, built a pine shelf and a cabinet for us to tangibly celebrate Ben's nineteen years, with exactly the result we were hoping for.

On Christmas Eve, David implemented a very meaningful touch in our church service. Anyone who was grieving the loss of a loved one was invited to come and light a tea-light candle and place it on a table at the front of the church as the rest of the congregation sang "Silent Night" softly in the background. Many responded, and David apologized for not thinking to do something like this sooner. However, no one can know what is appropriate until they have been there themselves.

A definite highlight occurred late on Christmas Eve when Natalie crawled between David and me in bed, and we gabbed about life and love into the wee hours of the morning. Although late, it was truly a special time shared with our oldest baby. And from my perspective, it set the tone for a wonderful family experience once we all arose on Christmas morning. We had Ben's lantern lit the entire day, which allowed us, in a very visual way, to remember and include the one we missed so much.

The first gifts we opened were pewter tree ornaments that a special friend of ours had given each of us in memory of Ben (each had the words "Merry Christmas from Heaven" engraved on them). Following that, we opened another gift from some other very special friends, who had each taken the time to write Ben a letter. Tears flowed naturally as our hearts were touched that others would enter into our grief so sensitively and meaningfully.

Friday, January 8, 2010: I Got Dressed Today!

I got dressed today! Yes, you read right. By this I mean that I was motivated to move beyond my "house clothes" to something I could actually venture to wear beyond my front door.

As David and I have compared notes to describe the way we're feeling, we've both used the same words. It's as if a blanket of sadness has been thrown over us in this winter season of our lives. I wouldn't go as far as to say that we're depressed, but neither of us is highly motivated. The anesthetic is wearing off. You'd think that as the months roll on and life begins to take the form of its new normal, we would grow more accustomed to the loss and all that goes with it. However, in many ways we're just now awakening to the pain of our reality.

Now, let me tell you why I got dressed today. David and I made a trip to the hospital where Ben was treated to visit our old hospital neighborhood, as well as our hospital family. It was wonderful to walk onto the floor and in each wing be warmly greeted by those we grew to love so deeply. Simultaneously every step, every visual reminder, and every encounter triggered such bittersweet memories. It is truly hard to imagine that *that* place was our home for an entire year. It was tough not just imagining but realizing that it truly was!

In keeping with my custom of claiming a Bible verse or passage for each new year, I thought I'd share the one for 2010. It is taken from Ecclesiastes 7. *"Don't long for the 'good old days,' for you don't know whether they were any better than today… Notice the way God does things; then fall into line. Don't fight the ways of God, for who can straighten out what he has made crooked? Enjoy prosperity while you can. But when hard times strike, realize that both come from God. That way you will realize that nothing is certain in this life"* (Ecclesiastes 7:10, 13–14, NLT).

Friday, January 29, 2010: The London Fog

"The London Fog" has fast become my new favorite winter drink. It's totally yummy, not to mention warm and soothing in my tummy! It consists of steamed milk, a hint of vanilla syrup, and an Earl Grey tea bag thrown in the mix to be brewed just so. It's total comfort and also where I feel I'm at right now. It's as if I'm living and breathing and functioning in an absolute fog. I'm forgetful, disoriented, easily distracted, single-minded, and most days blurry-eyed due to the tears that shroud my view so easily.

Some days, it seems the sky clears just a bit, enough for us to venture ahead at a less sluggish pace, while other days it takes a great deal more effort. Some days, we can hardly see our hands in front of our faces, let alone anything beyond it. So, as you can imagine, planning ahead is excruciating! One thing I've learned is the importance of heading to the mountainside with Jesus to just sit and simmer, allowing the fog to lift before attempting to plow ahead.

I know that eventually this London fog will lift and that there will be a spectacular view on the other side of the mountain. I have to believe that God has and will continue to use our pain to help others in theirs.

We wait, hopefully and patiently, for the clouds to clear.

Thursday, February 25, 2010: The Land of the Living

Last night, David and I had the opportunity to attend a bereavement workshop. One of the people on the panel was a young lady who lost her older brother five years ago. Something she said at the end of her presentation resonated with both David and me. She said that she has had to find ways to bring her brother into her life instead of bringing her into his death.

We, too, are on this quest and are finding it easier said than done. At least to this point, most memories of Ben continue to draw us back into his death, and we wonder some days if we will ever feel fully alive again without him. As morbid as it may be to some, in order to convince myself that Ben is really gone I have to relive the entire year, albeit in a matter of seconds, until I reach Ben's final days with us. It's after this still-frequent brain relapse that I'm vividly and sadly reminded that, *yes,* he is really dead.

Throughout Ben's illness, I prayed through and clung to Psalm 27:13–14, which says, *"I am still confident of this: I will see the goodness of the Lord in the land of the living. Wait for the Lord; be strong and take heart and wait for the Lord."* At the time, of course, I was hoping that "the land of the living" would signify God keeping Ben alive. Now knowing that that wasn't the case, what does this reference to "the land of the living" mean?

Months ago, I heard a quote that went like this: "Our mistake is we think that we are in the land of the living heading for the land of the dying when, in fact, those who have a personal relationship with Jesus are in the land of the dying heading for the land of the living."

We mistakenly live our lives on earth as if this is where the road ends. We need to realize that this place is a temporary home. There is a glorious inheritance awaiting our arrival in "the land of the living," where Ben is also awaiting us, more alive than he's ever been, that will far outweigh the pleasures we find here. If we can keep that in mind, I think we'll be well on our way to finding ways to bring him into our life rather than bringing ourselves into his death.

Lisa (Mom)

Lifeline

"Do not store up for yourselves treasures on earth, where moth and rust destroy, and where thieves break in and steal. But store up for yourselves treasures in heaven, where moth and rust do not destroy, and where thieves do not break in and steal. For where your treasure is, there your heart will be also" (Matthew 6:19–21).

Wednesday, March 17, 2010: Grief in the Raw

David and I have now had three sessions with our GriefShare group. One of the exercises encouraged us to write a letter to family and friends to express what our present state of grief is like and to let them know what to expect of us through this time. I shared my letter, in its very raw state, with the group while many nodded and appraised my words, obviously articulating what they were all feeling.

So here it goes, my "grief in the raw":

Dear Family and Friends,

Thank you for your love and support throughout this past year and a half with Ben's illness and subsequent death. It means so much to me, knowing you've carried me and my family on your knees in prayer to Jesus over and over again. Your practical expressions have also been so very much appreciated.

It's hard to imagine that it's been seven months since Ben changed addresses from his temporal home to his eternal home. It seems at times that it was just yesterday that he was running through the door on his way out again. And hence, it's still hard to believe that he is now gone and that there will no longer be memories that include him.

I know that it must be so painful for you to watch me in pain. I realize you may be at a loss for words or feel inadequate to reach into my pain. No doubt there are times when you feel awkward around me as I shed tears or at other times when I seem unresponsive to your attempts to somehow make me feel better. I thank you for your patience, as in my raw state of grief I may respond harshly to you. I apologize if in any way I have caused offense as I'm working through my grief.

I'm tired and easily distracted. I don't have a lot of social energy right now. In fact, in social settings I often feel like a caged animal looking for a quick escape route. I am sad, but I'm not looking for anyone to make me happy. I am broken, but I'm not looking for anyone to fix me. I am not looking for answers. I am not looking for sympathy. I need people to be okay with my sadness, realizing that my tears are bringing healing. I need people to be more interested in entering into my pain than trying to get me to the other side of it.

As much as I appreciate the loving motive behind them, assurances that "one day it'll all make sense" or "one day I'll feel better" only serve to project a future I can't make sense of yet. Words such as "Ben's in a better place" or "Ben isn't suffering any longer" don't bring the comfort that I'm seeking, but rather simply remind me of what I already know. Although they hold elements of truth, words intended to help me "look at the bright side" make me feel that somehow I'm living "on the dark side." Words that encourage me to think of "all I have to be thankful for," usually beginning with "at least…," only serve to minimize my pain and imply that I'm not thankful for what I do have. Words cheapen my pain. Answers to questions I'm not asking frustrate me.

Be assured that all is not destitute. There have been seconds that occasionally turn into moments where there is a vaguely recognizable sense of relief. I personally like how Ben's girlfriend, Sarah, described it in a recent conversation. She said, "It's like coming up for air. It's like most of the time we're in the ocean, and every once in a while we come up and take a quick breath of air before being submerged again." That revelation in and of itself was refreshing! Because, *yes*, grief can sometimes swallow you whole and suck the breath out of you!

I think all of us have done well to go on living life, even when it hurts. Just as God's grace sustained me and my family throughout Ben's illness, I know He will continue to do so now in our grief. God has strengthened us all to do the next thing… whatever that has been along the way. It might amount to something as simple as taking a walk or having an extra cup of tea, or just hanging together as a family.

God is comforting me with His quiet presence. He is holding my hand as He guides my steps. He is entering into my pain rather than seeking to get me over it. My pain is God's tool to reach deep into the recesses of my heart where He alone can speak powerful words of truth and comfort. I believe He is using my pain for His glory as I share my journey with others.

I don't know what "being okay" will look like for me personally, but I do know that I won't always feel as I do now. I know that laughter and joy will emerge again someday. And I do know that I will survive and eventually recover.

I cling to that knowledge even though there are times when I don't feel it. I trust that I will be a better person, becoming more like Jesus as a result.

Please pray that I will come to see meaning in my loss. Please pray that God will continue to teach me valuable lessons in my pain. Please feel free to talk to me and the rest of my family about Ben, and don't be afraid of our tears when you do. We long to hear mention of his name. We want to know that his life and death are still making an impact for the Kingdom of God. We want to know that he's not forgotten. Most of the time, given the right time and place, we are bursting to share our all-consuming thoughts with anyone who will give ear.

Thank you for caring about me and my family. Thank you for listening to me with no words. Thank you for validating my pain by simply crying with me. Thank you for understanding when I've seemed distant or aloof or disengaged or uninterested in your life. Thank you for giving me the necessary time and space to work through my grief. Thank you for not giving up on me.

And finally, *"Praise be to the God and Father of our Lord Jesus Christ, the Father of compassion and the God of all comfort, who comforts us in all our troubles, so that we can comfort those in any trouble with the comfort we ourselves have received from God"* (2 Corinthians 1:3– 4).

Lisa (Mom)

Things Not to Say

It's hard to know exactly what to say to someone in a crisis. Although people's intentions are good, they can say things that aren't helpful and can sometimes even be hurtful. (No doubt I have contributed to the list with my own "foot in mouth" disease.) Here are some of those things *not* to say.

- "_____ is in a better place." It may be true, but it's not helpful.
- "Don't worry! Everything will turn out just fine!" How do you know?
- "Just pray and everything will work out!" What if I'm angry at God? Or what if I'm already praying?
- "At least…" This minimizes the situation and the person's pain.
- "At least you have other children." Children are not interchangeable.
- "At least you can have other children." Children are not replaceable.
- "God wants healing." Yes, He does, but does He want healing here on earth or ultimate healing in heaven?
- "Don't go there." How can I *not* go there? Please just permit me to visit there without dwelling there.
- "Don't feel sad [mad, worried…]." Why not? That's the way I'm feeling!
- "What you need is…" You may be projecting a need of your own that isn't necessarily mine. Rather, put it into question form: "Is there anything you need that I can take care of for you?"
- "A friend of a friend of a friend of mine had the *exact* same thing!" Really? Every situation and circumstances surrounding the situation varies.
- "I know *exactly* how you feel!" Actually… no, you don't. You may be able to relate to a certain component of how I'm feeling, but don't ever assume to *totally* understand.

PRACTICAL TIPS (con't.)

- "Just have a good sleep and everything will look better in the morning." If only it were as easy as that!
- "Just stay positive! Look at the bright side." There is a difference between being optimistic and realistic.
- "God obviously felt He could entrust you with this pain." Does He have to trust me so much?
- "This was obviously God's will." Yes, God can bring good from it… but did He will it?
- "At least you had some time to prepare yourself for his death." The finality of death is entirely different than anticipatory grief.
- "Your loss is heaven's gain." My loss is still my loss.

Wednesday, April 21, 2010: Unseasonal Grief

No doubt the first question on everyone's minds will be "How was the Elliotts' time away?" And our answer in its simple form is "It was great." We enjoyed all we could, for as long as we could, as much as we could. David and Jacob took the opportunity to play an honorary "Ben-round" of golf that was gifted to them, while Erin and I opted to browse some shops. But as was to be expected, our grief didn't take a vacation. In fact, Ben's absence was more present than his presence would have been.

Our challenge was finding creative ways to handle our grief without stifling it or engulfing others in it. Erin got it off her chest right away at the first hotel we landed in as she struggled to get her mind around having a good "family vacation" without our entire family. Even I tried to convince myself that things might have been like this even if Ben were still alive, being off at university and such, but to no avail. There was no skirting around the truth of the matter: Ben will never again join us for a family vacation.

Believe me when I say that I would have loved nothing more than to report that our taste of summer and our welcome home to spring revived my soul and washed away all my sorrow. However, I must sadly report that while spring is in the air, it is still winter in my heart. I mildly resent that everything around me dictates that I should be happy and carefree, as it contradicts my heart, which still feels dead and cold. Fall and winter, with its drab and dreariness, more readily sang the tune of my grief. It suited my mellow mood. It naturally lent itself to my tendencies toward hibernation. Spring only heightens my awareness of "happy" people around me whose good intentions want nothing more than for me to be "happy" again.

One of the books of the Bible I reread while down in Myrtle Beach was Ecclesiastes. Verses in the third chapter say, *"There is a time for everything, and a season for every activity under heaven... a time to weep and a time to laugh, a time to mourn and a time to dance"* (Ecclesiastes 3:1, 4).

So, should I feel guilty for my defiance of spring? I don't think so. Having experienced winter seasons in my life before, I know that as much as everything seems lifeless during the winter, in reality there is much life taking place under the crust of the ice and snow. I know that winter is the season when God can do His work uninterrupted by life's activities and normal distractions.

Although my mood doesn't quite suit the season, I know that inevitably and in due season, spring will return to my heart, and I so look forward to that.

I'm still looking forward to spring!

Lifeline

"The God who made the world and everything in it is the Lord of heaven and earth and does not live in temples built by hands. And he is not served by human hands, as if he needed anything, because he himself gives all men life and breath and everything else. From one man he made every nation of men, that they should inhabit the whole earth; and he determined the times set for them and the exact places where they should live. God did this so that men would seek him and perhaps reach out for him and find him, though he is not far from each one of us. 'For in him we live and move and have our being'" (Acts 17:24–28).

Thursday, April 29, 2010: Getting to the Bottom of Things

The week we brought Ben home from the hospital, Susan, his nurse practitioner and one of Ben's number-one advocates, was away. Upon her return, I gave her a call to give her Ben's status. I told her that this wasn't quite what I had signed up for. I went on to tell her that Ben had been in a delusional state from the day we brought him home and wasn't eating or drinking much. Her response stuck with me: "It sounds like Ben has finally allowed himself to be sick."

I guess, in a sense, I have finally allowed myself to be sick by doing something I hadn't up until Good Friday, and I believe it will allow me to get healthy as a result. At our Good Friday service, I experienced the most brutal public display of emotion thus far. Although I was more than aware of Resurrection Sunday, I was having a rough time seeing past the cross that day. As we watched a DVD clip of a reenactment of Jesus' crucifixion, the scene of Jesus being carried down from the cross was replaced in my mind's eye with David and Jacob lifting and carrying Ben's lifeless body from his bed in our living room to the gurney that awaited him. And I heard Jesus' words from the cross in a way I'd never heard them before as He asked, "My God, my God, *why* have you forsaken me?" If you recall, He had already spent the previous evening wrestling with His Father in the Garden of Gethsemane, begging Him for there to be a way other than the cross. It struck me that, even knowing the answer, Jesus gave Himself permission to ask "Why?"

Even realizing that I may never know the answer, I took Jesus' "Why?" with me on our vacation. "Why did Ben have to die? Why did he even have to get sick? Why couldn't there have been another way to bring God the glory?"

You see, I've always been afraid to ask some of the tough questions, believing somehow that if I did, God would "forsake me," or at least that it would appear that I had forsaken Him. In fact, the opposite is true. Instead, I've discovered that asking God the hard questions has allowed Him to dig deeper into my soul with a deeper sense of healing. He wants truth in my innermost being!

I'm apparently not the only one who has asked some tough questions. That's what I love about the Psalms. They are brutally honest. I love that I can pour my heart out to God. I love that God can handle my raw state. I love that He can handle my questions. I love that He doesn't prevent me from asking them or judge me or criticize me when I do.

But I must admit, I'm looking forward to the coming day of redemption when all my questions will be answered. Everything will finally make sense. And who knows? Maybe when I finally see Jesus face to face, I won't even need to ask them!

Thursday, May 6, 2010: Exclamation Mark Moments!

I recently read the book of Ruth. After the loss of her husband and two sons, Ruth's mother-in-law changed her name from Naomi, meaning "pleasant," to Mara, meaning "bitter." I haven't gone as far as to change my name, but believe me when I tell you that I have occasionally been tempted to post a sign on my forehead that says "Grieving Mother. Approach at Your Own Risk!"

This is most prevalent every Sunday as I quickly make my way to my hideout in the back pew of our church. God, fortunately, has been helping me recognize how dangerous and unhealthy this could become. Unlike Naomi, I don't want to be remembered as "that woman who lost her son and never recovered." I don't want my grief to become my identity. Not only will it get me stuck in a stage of grief, but it could turn into a self-serving, self-absorbed life. It could also disengage me from many who are also grieving the loss of Ben and want nothing more than to come alongside me in my grief. Worse yet, it could stifle and even prevent the new life that God wants to accomplish in and through me out of the ashes of my grief—and that would be a tragic end to the Ben Ripple as it plays out in my life.

I felt really impressed to move beyond my back pew one particular Sunday to engage in conversation with a woman in our church. She'd had a stroke a few years ago that paralyzed one side of her body. I wanted to tell her how much her beautiful, godly attitude toward her affliction has inspired me as I've faced my own. We shared some tears with few words. God added His exclamation mark when she said, "Lisa, thank you for coming to me, because I can't come to you." Needless to say, God used her physical paralysis to lovingly prod me out of my self-preserving social paralysis.

Ben was never the victim in his illness. He chose to overcome it day after day. And that's what I intend to do as well. I'm not saying that my grief journey is over, but I want to choose life. I want to witness God's bigger picture as it unfolds. It's a decision and a choice I have to make every single day.

Lifeline

"Forget the former things; do not dwell on the past. See, I am doing a new thing! Now it springs up; do you not perceive it? I am making a way in the desert and streams in the wasteland" (Isaiah 43:18–19).

Tuesday, May 11, 2010: Loving by Letting Go

I received an email from a woman this past week expressing her condolences. She sensitively stated that, although she felt my pain, she didn't know what it is like to lose a child. However, instead of spelling it "lose," she put an extra "o" in to make it "loose." There is no way she could have realized just how profound her typo turned out to be, because rather than saying "My son died," I have found it easier to say "I lost my son." However, I realize now how very theologically incorrect I've been in my terminology. I haven't lost him at all. I know exactly where he is! He's in the arms of Jesus, being cared for better than I ever could! So, rather than telling people that I "lost" Ben, I should start telling them that I "loosed" him.

This leads me to the most recent question I've been asking God. "Can I still love Ben by letting him go?" The simple answer is, of course I can! I've been doing that from the time he was born. But this naturally leads me to yet another question: "*How* can I love Ben by letting him go?" This is one of the same questions I asked when I was pregnant with him. I wondered how I would ever love another child as much as I loved my firstborn, Natalie, and I'm finding that the answers are much the same. I simply learn to love him in a new way. I love him by grieving. I love him by remembering him. I love him by talking about him and thinking about him. I love him by missing him. And I also love him by looking forward to seeing him again one day, thanks to God's redeeming love for me.

It doesn't mean I love him any more or less than I love any of my other children. It's just that I now have to express my love for him in a new, more creative and intentional way. The fact still remains that whether it's Ben or Natalie or Jacob or Erin, I still have to learn to love them by letting them go!

Thursday, July 1, 2010: This Is Life

Yesterday would have been Ben's twentieth birthday. Many people have told me that the anticipation is often worse than the actual day or event. This is accurate, to a degree. It certainly doesn't take a special occasion to remind us of our daily reality. And in that way, no day is any worse than another. What makes these special occasions different than other days is the fact that they are punctuated. These are the days when others, who rightfully have gone on with their own lives, remember and enter into our loss with us.

We all set out to make the best of a day that we don't want to ever forget… the day that Benjamin David Elliott entered the world. Each of us, in our own way and in our own time, remembered.

As much as we made an award-winning attempt at celebrating Ben's life over ribs and were very much looking forward to our strawberry shortcake, none of us could get past the empty chair that more than ever accentuated his absence. Then David spotted a CD in the middle of the table. When he inquired about it, Natalie said that this was a birthday party and that we couldn't have a birthday party without a birthday present. With that, she put the CD into our CD player. We listened to a song that all three of our children, without our knowing, had written not only the lyrics to but also the music, including playing, performing, and professionally recording it for David and me.

Here are the words:

THIS IS LIFE
(Lyrics and music by Natalie, Jacob, and Erin Elliott)

Feel the warmth of the covers, a backrub, a mother's prayers,
A lullaby to calm her little boy.
Just before he falls asleep, she leans down to kiss his cheek.
Then she softly whispers in his ear…

Son, this is life. Can you feel it ripple through you?
Feel the love of the One who will always be true.
He's in your dreams, He's in your prayers, He's all around just, cast your cares.
He wants to use you… Son, this is life.

Feel the spray of cold water, a tin boat, a son and father
Set out to find adventure on the bay.
Fishing poles, a can of worms, excited laughter, then some words,
The boy leans in to hear his father say…

Son, this is life. Can you feel it ripple through you?
Feel the love of the One who will always be true.
He's in the wind, He's in the waves, He's in your heart, He's there to stay.
He's calling to you… Son, this is life.

(Do not fear, our God is with you)
'Cuz though my heart and flesh may not endure. And life gets hard, of this I'm sure:
(Do not fear, He's here!)
Our God, He does not fail, He is the cure!
Feel the love of the Father, see heaven's gates and all the colors,
Walking hand in hand with the One who made it all.
Sing with the angels, laugh and smile, I sure do miss you, It's been a while.
Just close your eyes and you can hear me say…

This is life. Can you feel it ripple through you?
Feel the love of the One who will always be true.
I've heard His voice, I've seen His face, I'm now healed fully by His embrace.
I know I'll see you soon… This is life![2]

Psalm 73:26 says, *"My flesh and my heart may fail, but God is the strength of my heart and my portion forever."*
What more can I add?

• • •

---

[2] A video of "This Is Life" can be viewed on YouTube. Just search for "This Is Life, The Elliotts."

The Ben Ripple

Wednesday, July 28, 2010: Ode to Joy

These past few weeks, and as we draw closer to the one-year anniversary of when Ben changed addresses, David and I have been incredibly sad. This past Sunday, in particular, for no specific reason was extremely sad and emotional for me. It wasn't my typical tidal wave of emotion. Rather, it was more like a tsunami, and it took me under for most of the day. But for those of you who are worried that I've lost my joy, have no fear. I find her every Sunday at church! In fact, she saves me a seat in the back row and remains with me until the last person has left. Joy has been a gift to me. Let me describe her to you:

Joy understands the pain of losing someone you love. Joy lost her father fourteen years ago this past Sunday.

Joy told me on Sunday that some days it's easier to just be numb, because to feel is to be in pain. I thought that was very profound.

Joy also knows that God can only heal pain when we allow ourselves to feel it.

Joy is soft-spoken and a woman of few words, but her presence assures me that no words can reach into the deep places of my heart that are meant for God alone.

Joy gives me the time and space I need to meet God in my pain.

Joy stands aside and doesn't interfere with what God is doing in the deep inner recesses of my heart.

Joy doesn't try to fix me. Joy has no words of advice for me. Joy just listens. She fully realizes that God alone can give the kind of healing I need.

Joy is okay with my pain.

Joy knows full well that sometimes there are just no words to describe my pain.

Joy lets me be real about my raw feelings and doesn't leave my side just because I'm having a bad day.

Joy reminds me that although the pain never fully goes away, it will get easier to deal with in time.

Joy assures me that eventually I will remember happy memories of Ben with a smile on my face and not just a tear in my eye.

Joy demonstrates to me that life can go on, making new memories and learning new things about God as I do.

Joy rejoices with me and my small baby-step victories.

Joy has told me that it's okay to want to be alone to rest, recover, and take the necessary time to heal.

Joy has warned me to be real about my pain and not try to conceal it.

Joy celebrates the ways that God is using my pain to reach others and sees the potential of the ripple effect in and through my life.

Joy allows me to worship through my tears.

Joy sings alongside me and my pain in beautiful harmony.

Joy lets me be sad when I'm with her and has shown me firsthand that joy and pain can truly coexist.

Joy sounds an awful lot like another joy I know—the joy of the Lord. Yes, I have grown to love the person Joy, but she would be the first one to remind me that it is the joy of the Lord that is my strength (Nehemiah 8:10).

This is my "Ode to Joy."

Lifeline

"I tell you the truth, you will weep and mourn while the world rejoices. You will grieve, but your grief will turn to joy" (John 16:20).

Monday, August 9, 2010: Lest We Forget

After Ben passed away, I went on a mission of madness. I moved all of Jacob's things into Natalie's room, thinking that this would be easier on him than going back into the room that he and Ben had always shared. I also moved all of Ben's things, which he had meticulously "put into order" a couple of weeks earlier, down into our basement. In twenty-four hours, it was done!

There was a method to my madness. I figured, *Out of sight, out of mind,* that by putting Ben's things in the basement I could hide all evidence of his existence and, therefore, alleviate my pain.

What made it difficult was that David's greatest fear following Ben's death was that somehow he would forget him. So while I was busy burying anything and everything that would trigger memories, David was doing anything and everything to keep Ben's memory alive. He invited me to listen to grief CDs, read grief books, look at pictures of Ben, and relive moments from the previous year. For me, it felt like nothing more than an exercise in emotional torture. David, however, was finding healing by choosing to remember.

Fortunately, I've realized the error of my ways. I've since learned that remembering is a significant part of my healing.

The Ben Ripple

Deuteronomy 8:11–15 are some of my favorite verses: *"Be careful that you do not forget the Lord your God... Otherwise, when you eat and are satisfied, when you build fine houses and settle down, and when your herds and flocks grow large and your silver and gold increase and all you have is multiplied... you will forget the Lord your God... He led you through the vast and dreadful desert, that thirsty and waterless land"* (emphasis added).

Not only does Deuteronomy warn us not to forget, but we are encouraged to remember! I don't ever want to *forget* Ben and the significant role he played in our nineteen years together. More importantly, I want to *remember* what God has taught me, especially through this wilderness time in my life. I want to be able to tell my children's children about their Uncle Ben and his love for Jesus. I want them to hear about all the miracles God performed during his illness and thereafter. I want them to take note of God's sustaining power and grace.

Lest we forget.

PRACTICAL TIPS

Creative Ways to Honor Your Loved One

One of our greatest fears was forgetting about Ben. We were, therefore, desperate to uncover some ways in which we could honor his memory. The following are a few ways we either came across or put into place ourselves. Making memories and honoring our loved ones is very personal, and therefore will be different for everyone.

- Make a picture album or scrapbook of family memories.
- Create a display area in your home.
- Make some kind of special garden.
- Plant a tree.
- Put fresh flowers next to a special picture.
- Think of something you can do to celebrate special occasions (birthday, Christmas, etc.).
- A special meal.
- A Christmas ornament.
- Put together a special picture frame with a special picture.
- Dedicate a bench with an engraved plaque in a strategic spot.
- Develop a charitable event (golf tournament, marathons, medical-related events) in your loved one's honor.
- Set up a fund or scholarship that will go toward others in a similar crisis. For instance, we set up the BENevolent Fund.
- Write a letter to the deceased.
- Create a special memorial room.
- Write a song or poem.
- Find a special place for significant personal items (favorite hats, watch, blanket).
- Make a CD of your loved one's favorite music.
- Invest in a candle or lantern that can be lit on special occasions or "missing moments" to acknowledge your loved one's absence.
- Make a "memory quilt" with pieces of your loved one's clothing, pictures, and clichés they would have said.

PRACTICAL TIPS (con't.)

- Design a special T-shirt or logo.
- Dedicate something to the hospital or facility where your loved one was cared for. For example, we donated money toward some necessary bed-chairs for the cancer ward.
- Write a book!

Wednesday, August 11, 2010: The Victory Bell

The victory bell is a small library bell that patients ring following their final treatment at the cancer clinic. Ben was never too impressed with this bell and its little "tinker." He said that when his turn came, he wanted to ring a different bell—and he had just the right one in mind. He knew of an old gonging fire bell that was being discarded at the toy store he'd worked at, so he promptly sought it out. It was his idea to present this bell at the end of his treatment and be the first one to ring it.

Ben never did ring the victory bell. Rather, it remained safely tucked away in his bedroom closet until I found it while sorting through his things after he left this earth.

David and I made it our mission last fall to see Ben's wish fulfilled by personally delivering the bell to the clinic. While patients still refer to it as the victory bell, nurses lovingly call it "The Ben Bell."

Although Ben didn't personally get to ring it, we believe he won the victory in every way. First of all, he chose never to play the victim throughout his illness, right up to his last breath. Secondly, he's living victorious over death and the grave because of his unashamed profession of faith in the Lord Jesus Christ. This past Sunday marked the day that, a year ago on August 9, Ben gave his "victory speech" as he stood in our church pulpit only ten days before he died.

The timing of this significant day in history also turned into a significant day in our grief journey. On Sunday, David preached from Revelation 2 about suffering, death, and heavenly reward—not unlike Ben's message the year before. He told us what it is to be a true victor—or "overcomer," as it is referred to in Revelation. At the end of the message, David felt it appropriate to play the DVD of Ben's talk. As a result, four people committed their lives to Jesus. If that's not a Ben Ripple, I don't know what is! It's proof enough to me that, like Abel, "*by faith [Ben] still speaks, even though he is dead*" (Hebrews 11:4).

We rejoice in all the ways that God is still using Ben's life and death to ripple out. While we don't expect that anything will ever replace Ben, ripples like this put a healing salve on the wound. This week marks two years since Ben's diagnosis and next week will mark one whole year that he has been gone from our lives. And by God's grace and minute-by-minute strength, we have survived. I feel like we should be running down to the cancer clinic and gonging the Ben Bell! And maybe we will!

185

The Ben Ripple

Wednesday, August 18, 2010: B.B.

David and I have been spending a lot of time on our backyard garden swing this summer. We often have a coffee in hand, using our time alone together to connect and also share in our grief while we watch the birds. Rising earlier than the rest of us, David has also grown accustomed to bringing his Bible and our family grief journal outside with him where he can spend some uninterrupted time with the Lord and with Ben in his thoughts to begin his day.

In his last days with us, Ben loved to be able to come into the backyard, where we made our swing into a bed for him. It took great effort to get him there, as he couldn't walk farther than two or three feet without taking a break, so one of us would escort him and the other would follow close behind with a stool for him to rest on. It was worth every ounce of effort just to see Ben soaking in the precious moments that were coming quickly to an end. One day, he spent six hours out there just basking in the peace and quiet. Although his eyesight was growing dim, he could still see colors, so he especially loved watching the goldfinches feeding with their brilliant yellow feathers.

So it only made sense that God used a "feathered friend" to minister to us during the week of what would have been Ben's twentieth birthday. A bird of a different breed landed on my doorstep just yesterday during this first anniversary of Ben's death.

Let me tell you first about the birthday bird. This was no ordinary bird. Not only was he an unknown variety compared to the many we host at our feeders, but this bird seemed drawn to us personally. In fact, he would fly in from out the blue as soon as one of us entered the backyard! It was as if he was perched somewhere close-by, just waiting for our arrival.

The relationship developed as he seemed more interested in our company than the birdseed! He got so friendly that he even began attempting to fly up onto our laps!

We grew so accustomed to his company that we finally named him B.B.—an abbreviation for "Ben's Bird," believing that God had sent him our way to put a smile on our faces. We began feeding him specialty foods for variety sake, and he took quite a liking to watermelon. We didn't offer any tacos, which was one of Ben's favorites. His final dinner with us was some nacho chips with guacamole, which he thoroughly enjoyed.

One night, David and I were enjoying a nice dinner el fresco. B.B. took the notion and hopped right up onto the middle of the table, where he perched himself on my wire-framed candle stand. There he sat while we ate our entire

dinner. He of course entered into our table talk, too. When David laid his cut-
lery down at the completion of his dinner, B.B. boldly moved to his plate and
finished off the tidbits. B.B. remained with us for the entire week. We haven't
seen him since.

It is amazing that God would take such interest in us to send a no-name bird
to keep us company during the week of Ben's birthday. It was no less amazing
that this week, the anniversary of Ben's home-going, an airmail delivery flew in
and landed on my doorstep. It was a gift from a special friend whom I have yet
to meet face to face. The gift she sent was a Willow Tree angel. Amazingly, this
particular angel (called the Angel of Healing) is holding a bird. The second that
I showed my family, my girls both responded by saying, "Look! She's holding
B.B." Who but God would know how to minister to my heart so significantly?

I hope I never cease to be amazed at God's intimate love for me or His significantly detailed interest in my life… especially during times of brokenness and
drought.

Lifeline

"Look at the birds of the air… Are you not much more
valuable than they?" (Matthew 6:26).

• • •

Through my journey of grief, I've come to agree with the words of the great
philosopher Charlie Brown: "I used to take each day as it came, but my philoso-
phy has changed. I'm down to half a day at a time." Some days, it's more like one
hour at a time, one minute at a time, or even one step at a time. I also appreciate the words of the Psalmist, indicating that some days it's simply going *"from
strength to strength"* (Psalm 84:7).

In light of the journey I've been on, I can't help but consider the surrounding
verses, which say, *"Blessed are those whose strength is in you, who have set their hearts
on pilgrimage. As they pass through the Valley of Baca, they make it a place of springs;
the autumn rains also cover it with pools. They go from strength to strength, till each
appears before God in Zion"* (Psalm 84:5–7, emphasis added).

In researching these verses, I found out that the pilgrimage to the temple
had to pass through the barren Valley of Baca, which can mean "weeping." My
pilgrimage to meet God in my grief has certainly been nothing less. However, I
also know that *"weeping may remain for a night, but rejoicing comes in the morn-*

ing" (Psalm 30:5). The challenge can be getting through the night—and it can prove to be a test in endurance.

I'm reminded of when I was a young mother of four children under the age of five and a half. It wasn't hard to lose sight of the enjoyment factor during that particular season of life. I was often told that "These days will be gone before you know it." But at times, it was all I could do just to get through a given day. That is, until an elderly man I loved and respected, who had raised six children of his own, told me, "Lisa, God gave us our children to *enjoy,* not simply to *endure.*"

I've never forgotten those words. In fact, I considered them to be so profound that I used them as a guiding principle as I raised my children. Since then, I've discovered that this principle has a much broader application. God gave me *life* to enjoy, not simply endure. However, it's easy to lose sight of this principle when life becomes an endurance test, such as the one I've been through since Ben's death. It's hard to live the abundant life when the life is sucked out of you, and yet I know that God doesn't want me to simply endure the rest of my days on this earth. He truly wants me to enjoy Him and all that He has blessed me with.

It's not unlike a message Ben left us on a CD he made in his final days. He entitled the CD "Ben's Seven Important Songs" and wanted it used at his funeral. David and I had not listened to Ben's CD until the day after his death. We discovered a long pause following one of the songs, so each time we listened to it, we skipped to the next song, thinking that it was a mistake. However, one day when we were too preoccupied by the emotion of making funeral arrangements, we didn't fast-forward. Needless to say, we were taken by surprise when out of the blue a happy tune began to play, telling us to "Have Fun in Life."

We believe that Ben recorded it purposely, knowing that there would come a day when we would have to be reminded of the need to learn to *enjoy* life again without him.

So, with Ben's prompting and by God's grace, we will make our way from strength to strength until we appear before Him. And until then, we're learning to once again not simply endure, but to have fun in life.

Epilogue
STUNNING CONCLUSION

Where and how do I begin to write the conclusion to a story that is still being written?

You have now walked with me through a year of the gradual and painful loss of my son Ben, with all its twists and turns. You have grieved and mourned with me since his death. I will never again be referred to as "Ben's Mom," and nothing and nobody will ever replace that loss. But that doesn't mean the story doesn't have an ending; nor does it mean that the ending isn't a happy one.

When my four kids were small and hurt themselves, they would come running to me with tears, in pain, and with a groaning that they couldn't always immediately put into words. I would take them into my arms, sit them on my lap until the heaving sobs had subsided, and tell them that everything would be okay, even as hard as it was for them to believe at the time.

It's hard to imagine what "okay" looks like when you're in pain.

I can't help but think that this is what heaven will be like. I picture myself running into the open arms of my heavenly Father when I finally see Him face to face for the first time. I can picture my tears of sadness flowing freely down my face, along with all my pain, loss, complaints, questions, and groaning that have no words. I also picture the tears of relief and joy that I will experience when He takes me into His arms and holds me in His embrace until my heaving sobs subside. When that time comes, He will make everything okay. I will be filled with a feeling of satisfaction, perspective, and comfort unlike anything I've never known before.

The Ben Ripple

I have to believe that I will experience an even more satisfying relationship with Ben in our eternal heavenly home than the one we shared here in our earthly home. I have to believe, like the hymn-writer of long ago, that "it will be worth it all when we see Jesus. Life's trials will seem so small when we see Christ."[3] Or, as in the words of the Apostle Paul, *"Now we see but a poor reflection as in a mirror; then we shall see face to face. Now I know in part; then I shall know fully, even as I am fully known"* (1 Corinthians 13:12).

So you see? There really is a happy ending! I believe it will be one that far exceeds anything I can think or imagine in the here and now. In fact, there is no doubt in my mind that it will be a stunning conclusion! I am looking forward to that day, but for now I will continue to allow God to write the rest of the story.

Letting it ripple,

Lisa (Mom)

---

[3] Esther Kerr Rusthoi, "When We See Christ," 1941.

In Memory of Ben